The Cats' Hotel, a safe and special place in England, is like a feline magnet where homeless, hungry and sometimes ill cats are attracted and have their lives transformed within its caring environment. The Cats' Hotel relates the individual true stories of fifteen cats, told with humour, which will appeal to cat lovers of all ages.

With 175 illustrations you can read about their contrasting personalities and their quirks, crazy adventures and (sometimes) mishaps. Despite their differences, as in any social group, individual roles and strengths are revealed resulting eventually in compromise, harmony and understanding.

Enjoy your visit to The Cats' Hotel!

The Cats' Hotel

Pamela Blanchfield

15 cats' stories

175 illustrations

With thanks

I would like to give very special thanks to my brother John Blanchfield, who has given invaluable, patient technical advice and guidance, without whose skill this book would not have been possible.

I also wish to give appreciative thanks to Rob Linnstedt for his continual support and frequent help in caring for our lovely hotel friends, and me.

Last but certainly not least, I have to offer sincere gratitude to our fantastic, kind, exceptionally long-suffering and wonderful vet, Nigel Griffiths.

This book is dedicated to
Clifford James Mouat,
my friend, in profound appreciation.

All text and illustrations copyright ©Pamela Blanchfield 2022 All rights reserved.

No part of this publication may be reproduced, stored in a retrieval system, stored in a database and / or published in any form or by any means, electronic, mechanical, photocopying, recording or otherwise, without the prior written permission of the publisher.

Contact: sales@keyprints.plus.com

ISBN: 978-1-3999-3415-2

Contents

- The Cats' Hotel 3
- With thanks 4
- This book is dedicated to 4
- Lively Leonora 7
- Gentle Jasper 21
- Reserved Roland 31
- Melancholy Marley 41
- Nifty Tufty 51
- Tenacious Tuppence 61
- Badger Brock 73
- Wonderful Woody 86
- Intrepid Elfie 99
- Clever Chester 115
- Filthy Wilfy 125
- Squeaky Chiki 137
- Queen Talitha 147
- Moody Maria 159
- Winsome Lucy 167
- The Cats' Hotel Series 176
- About the author and illustrator Pamela Blanchfield 177

Lively Leonora
Our fickle, friendly extrovert

Like a tiny tabby princess, Leo's intelligent, bright young eyes peered out from the safety of her tartan-lined carriage, and, surrounded by a cloak of auburn curls, she wondered where her travels in Donny's duffle coat hood might take them today. Fascinated by bird-watching and no stranger to the seaside, this happy kitten had a very unusual and varied routine. A familiar sight near their home, warm smiles often greeted the pair: "How are you two this morning?" "Where are you both off to now?"

Today, though heavy showers were inconveniently frequent and little Leonora looked doubtfully at Donny: "Where will we go in this rain?" "Well Leo! I think we shall visit Henry and Polly and their cats; jump on board!" And bobbing along, several smiling 'hellos' later, another exciting visit beckoned, but, later, just as they were leaving to head back home, she heard Donny, in hushed tones, talking: "Is that alright with you then? Leo does love your cats and is always happy here. I'll be back down from the Scottish Highlands in three weeks".

Watching Donny stride off, he waved and called "Au revoir!" then he was gone from sight. It was only later Leo's mood brightened – but not for very long. A horrible feeling of unease began to overwhelm her, and although only a youngster, she knew feelings were very important. It wasn't Henry and it wasn't Polly: they made nearly as much fuss of her as Donny always did. "Something about the cats that live here isn't right", decided Leonora, "I have to leave too!" Impelled and invisibly, the lodger promptly disappeared.

Naturally puzzled when Leo vanished, soon after the couple were otherwise preoccupied, and urgently calling their vet, seriously concerned, their own youngest cat was suddenly gravely ill. And, despite their taking swift action sadly nothing at all helped the kitten. Within a short time they now had two, not three cats. Then the worst imaginable event took place: both older cats also became unwell, declining rapidly over the coming weeks and even the vet couldn't save them. Distressed, they dug the last grave, lit a candle and tearfully remembered the lovely cats they had lost.

Nine gloomy days later, as he stood alone in the garden by the little sombre place full of memories, Henry unexpectedly caught sight of a pretty, familiar face: "Leo?" Out she trotted and, pausing at the precise spot, ran towards him looking fine and extremely well despite being away for nearly three weeks.

Another bright face appeared shortly after: it was Donny, back home from Scotland, and, wearing his duffle coat, broadly smiling, he collected his clever kitten, and nestled once again in his cosy, familiar hood, they sauntered home united, a team again.

Young Leonora enjoyed life once more, spending the next few months travelling around with fabulous Donny. There were visits to friends, lots of lazing in sunny summer fields, exciting coastal trips and regular walks around the lakes in the big park. "Everything is perfect" thought Leo, who was now almost nine months old. "Donny is the best person ever!" But what Leo didn't know was that Donny had wanderlust: however many miles Donny walked he still had 'itchy feet' and the urge to travel was even stronger than his love for little Leo.

"Where are we off to Donny?" but, Leo noticed, today Donny didn't reply, look at her or even smile. Mystified, she then saw he was quietly gathering her things together: toys, feeding bowls, blanket, all went swiftly into a bag: "Hop up precious!"

Today Donny was strolling very slowly, along lanes that Leo didn't know, and, strangely, he didn't speak again until they arrived at an unfamiliar front door. "I have a special present for you!" Donny, beaming, informed the woman who answered his knock. And holding the kitten, he carefully passed her into the new and inviting arms, and then announced: "I am off to India soon!" Instantly the young cat was welcomed, and the woman smiled widely: "Ooooh! Really? For me?! Thank you Donny! What a beautiful kitten: she looks so intelligent! This is the most wonderful present I have ever received! I am delighted. Thank you!" which immediately made Leo feel very much better. "Her name is Leonora, although I often call her Leo and actually she was born under the star sign of Gemini!" Donny explained, and after a chat, down the path he strode with a cheery wave calling "Au revoir!"

"This must be my lucky day!" the woman smiled and stroked Leo, who, reassured, soon restfully snuggled in a delightful new bed and drifted dreamily off to sleep.

And before long, being very adaptable as well as clever, Leo thought: "Now I can meet lots of new people on my own!" And it was true – she soon found many new friends nearby and the local cats liked Leonora too. Her charisma never failed.

Some happy months later the woman noticed Leo was looking rather plump, and although still a kitten, realised she was going to have a litter herself. A nest was prepared in a safe, warm space within an open cupboard and lined with a few old jumpers for reassurance.

Arriving home one evening after a short while away, the woman knew Leo was waiting for her return and soon after two kittens were born in her ready-prepared nook: a short-haired tabby and a little black and white one. Offering words of encouragement, Leo looked quite content settled with her six-hour-old kittens, so the woman stroked her and said "Goodnight, well done", and went to bed.

The next morning a really big surprise had

joined the two cute kittens: a fluffy long-haired tabby, and astonishingly he was almost twice as large, very handsome, huge, and with massive paws! Leo appeared to be shocked too: he looked as though he'd come from another, much older litter! Size though, as they say, is not everything and it soon became clear that Roland (as he was later called) - was rather reluctant to leave his nest. After a while his brother and sister started to get more adventurous, but Roland definitely wasn't like them. Unwilling to eat solid food, he didn't want to explore or use the litter tray and hung on to Leo, refusing to join in the rough-and-tumble games the other two enjoyed. This seemed quite puzzling, given his size, which might have suggested a more advanced kitten: all he wanted was to be with his Mum. So it was then decided Roland would perhaps be happier staying at the hotel.

However, there was one problem that had never been anticipated! It soon became apparent that Roland and Leo were not on the same wavelength at all. The momentous day came when he did eventually leave the safety of the nest - but later it was speculated whether perhaps he was actually evicted?!

Strangely, as he grew, although otherwise placid by nature, he began to develop a threatening stance and scowl directed solely at Leo. Roland quickly realised this was always guaranteed to send his mother scurrying off panic-stricken and an odd pattern developed. As soon as Leo is evidently feeling sufficiently scared, he enthusiastically, menacingly chases her as she vaults over furniture and obstacles wildly leaping in her fright to escape. Leo then glares furiously at him from lofty perches; and exchanging very mean looks (but never actually coming to blows), her speedy reaction and agility are truly tested every time. This naughty sport is reserved solely for his mother - a very confident cat who is never apparently intimidated by others! Maybe due to Roland's large size, Leo had experienced some difficulty in giving birth to him, especially as she was only a youngster and still quite petite, and combined with her impatience and obvious frustration at Roland's slow development, it was wondered later if ultimately this had perhaps caused such a curiously confrontational situation.

Leo usually escapes into the garden, knowing "He won't chase me out here"; and, loving being outside, she observes everything: the birds in the trees, the fox holes in the garden and intrigued, spends many exciting, fun hours gazing into the pond.

Slightly dubious about the practicality of rescuing some indoor goldfish – the woman surreptitiously placed the tank in an out-of-the-way spot whispering "Is Leo out?" But less than a week passed before the small, perceptive cat had nimbly found her way up despite the obstacles placed in her way. Caught in the act, Leo, precariously perched on that very high, inaccessible shelf, with a paw in the water merrily fishing, had a fascinated, wicked glint in her eyes: "Is this a gift for me – my very own fish pond indoors?" Urgently the tank of fish was removed and swiftly re-homed once again!

Very affectionate, and never slow to reinforce the case with needle-sharp claws accompanied by a loud, rumbling, whistling purr, Leo's privileged friends experience her happy, busy feet and vigorous knee puncturing; gazing brightly she will always say "YOU are my favourite person!" Despite the many trees outside (quite adequate for other cats), Leo's claws are honed to perfection from choice on rows of books, and many tattered volumes stand distressed, in witness to this unfortunate pursuit.

But Leonora is both highly sociable and cannily shrewd and those claws are an essential part of gaining access to her many selected haunts!

Never shy about nimbly nipping through neighbours' windows and open doors to gain entry to human's beds or linen cupboards, her strategy was cunningly perfected: if she finds her chosen entrances closed, Leo's contingency plan comes into play! Rapidly and vigorously clawing at glass windows, frowning crossly, producing an awful screeching sound like nails on a chalk board, the humans inside dash with jangling nerves to make sure they are immediately opened, and her various friends quickly admit their visitor like an honoured guest!

One dark winter's evening, a neighbour, a pianist called Graham, decided to pop out to the nearest shop leaving his girlfriend Jayne at home, alone, reading in their bedroom. She listened to his car leave and all was quiet and still in the big old house,

until Jayne, instantly alarmed, heard notes spookily being played on the piano. Rigid with fear and imagining visions of a ghostly, avant-garde piano player from another time, she sat shaking, rooted anxiously immobile in the chair. As soon as Graham returned, he was greeted not only by a wildly hysterical, tearful girlfriend, but a bold, familiar and friendly cat: "I just love visiting here! I slipped past you when you left, but I'm not sure you saw me! And, by the

way! Thank you for leaving your piano lid up: it's so exciting! I've had great fun, so is it alright if I play something else now?"

The ultimate feline extrovert, an over-heated human calling at the hotel on a hot day will delight Leo's delicate nostrils. Sniffing loudly, "Mmmmmpurrrmmmm!" she burrows excitedly into odorous armpits, burying her head in a frenzied purring rapture. This can take the (often, blushing) unsuspecting summer-day-damp visitor a little by surprise. And purr! If there was a Cat Purring Championship, her ecstatic, high-volume vibrations would surely bring home the medals!

Just like a student who has an important essay to write, Leo avidly watches all the wildlife programmes on TV with rapt concentration. She is a cat who possesses many talents: friends and callers are always guaranteed a thrilling acrobatic display by this agile gymnast. Places other cats might avoid become vaulting perches for Leo – ledges and banisters, open steps and awkward, high tree branches: she jumps and twists and twirls and leaps, pirouetting from platform to precarious perch in her wildly captivating circus act. Drawing astonished, admiring comments and applause, the clapping from her entranced audience sees Leo totally in her element basking in the attention.

A genial, diverse mixer, often Leo is found outside the hotel grounds in the lane being fussed over by groups of children and a familiar "hello" will be completely ignored in favour of them! This fickle friend mingles entirely on her own terms though, and her super-sharp claws are always ready to teach any rough children a cautionary lesson!

Vases of cut flowers decorated the hotel – before Leo arrived! With a peculiar fetish and apparent relish, she chewed the petals to shreds, resulting in a very odd-looking cat with green teeth and a pollen-orange-nose; and this very bizarre, unwise pursuit resulted in the end of floral displays (many flowers are dangerous if eaten by a cat). Houseplants too are not immune: Leo leaves the motley evidence of sadly perforated, stunted greenery. Spending hours enjoying adventures in the grounds, she has free access to a variety of grasses and plants, but curiously, somehow none seem to appeal quite as much!

Oddly, Leo likes to lick slugs: a guaranteed stomach-turner for the average person! And, being a very affectionate cat, often once back indoors, she then can't resist the intimacy of sharing a jumper being worn by the woman. Eagerly thrusting her head and wriggling underneath the waistband, with absolutely no regard for shape or style, she will burrow and squirm up the inside, and, stretching it to accommodate the wearer plus a friendly cat, her loudly purring head will triumphantly emerge from the neckline. Often, as this cosy

encounter is accompanied by joyful nose-rubbing, the woman will say "Yes, you are very beautiful and no, I really am NOT thinking of slugs!" Unusually considerate and just prior to bringing up a fur ball or being sick, Leo gives a high-pitched clarion crescendo call of warning: "Ow wow ow wow ow wow ow WOWOOW!" – allowing just ten seconds for a human to grab the kitchen roll! Lithe, trim and, thankfully, seldom ill, this is fortunate because Leo has a distinct aversion to all medication. She'll resist furiously with super strength, spitting and hissing with fierce determination, her unearthly howling showing a strongly-marked distrust of the pill intended for her throat. Even when zipped into a leather bag as a last resort, with only her disgruntled protesting head visible, her prima donna performance continues (usually without any success at all), earning her the title: 'worst ever patient at the Cats' Hotel'!

Leo's a wonderful, incredibly intelligent, gregarious cat who always enchants, entertains, surprises and amuses people. Captivating kittens, Leo is always the first to introduce herself to any new arrivals at the hotel who are fastidiously washed, played with and then patiently watched over by this energetic and ever-willing kitten-sitter. She cares for and loves other cats very much – all cats except for one: her big son, Roland.

Gentle Jasper
Our precious, brave guardian

He was alone: suddenly, completely alone. The cosy nest which so recently had bustled with the furry, jostling warmth and chatter of his littermates, his big, boisterous brothers and sisters and caring mother, now only contained the frightened, lonely black kitten. Peter gazed at him glumly, then removing his spectacles and rubbing his eyes with the back of his hand, scratching his head, he sighed loudly and spoke: "Oh Suzie, what will we do? I was so pleased the kittens were all going to good homes and now we only have the little runt that no one has come for. It's so sad, such a shock, now he tragically doesn't have his mother anymore either: it's bleak." Her eyes filled with tears as she tried to register the contrasting scene, so empty and hopeless from the one very happy day before.

Stroking the under-sized kitten, sitting by itself and now looking even smaller in isolation, she turned to Peter, and with a hint of optimism, said: "I'm hoping for a miracle: the advert is still in the corner shop" and the instant she said 'shop", her phone rang. "Peter! The lady wants a friend for her young female cat! She likes black cats and is coming straightaway!"

One glimpse of the diminutive but lovely kitten met her full approval, and excitedly whisking him into her arms the woman pronounced firmly "perfect!" And confidently: "What he most needs now is a furry friend, lots of love and a good home, and I know exactly the right place!" As if fully understanding her bright words, the kitten murmured, then readily snuggled into her furry coat lining, and delighted, closely holding the tiny cat, she beamed broadly, and even Suzie and Peter both smiled together. Then, after paying a contribution to thank the couple, the woman and the purring kitten set off happily back to the hotel and all the way there they chattered cheerfully to each other. She quickly, instinctively called him Jasper. And because he has the curious distinction of 'being bought' – (unlike all the other hotel residents who have made their own way, were found, or brought here) – seemed later very appropriate when discovering that the rare and valued gemstone black jasper sometimes contains gold. The woman often whispers to lovable, affectionate Jasper: "You are my treasured gem, and worth lots more than even gold!"

Jasper was instantly appealing, and, cuddling up inside her warm coat as they walked along, purring with pleasure, he straight away began to chew her long hair. Perfect, but very small to begin with, and looking much too young to be without his mother, she soon realised she'd been adopted and promoted to that surrogate role.

Jasper's favourite place was established quickly: stretched up over the woman's shoulder happily chewing her hair. Unfortunately his very active claws swiftly began to remodel her fancy, stylish clothes: "Cashmere! Damask silk! Lovely! Velvet! So soft and reassuring!" and the kitten padded away, paws-ever-busy – his furiously frisky, sharp claws, merrily shredding, whilst happily drooling, blissfully oblivious to the tattered evidence! "Oh! Never mind – this is an embroidered antique jacket, now somewhat distressed, but it could start a new look, and, after all – they're only clothes, so combined with my usual coating of various coloured cat hairs, I'll tell myself I'm the honorary hotel cat," remarked the woman to herself, resigned.

Immediately Jasper was introduced to Leo he was eagerly greeted with enthusiasm and affection, which he fondly reciprocated, and wisely and willingly, she patiently began to teach him the things a young cat usually learns from his mother. Leo instantly became Jasper's special pal, and he was encouraged by her to play.

Over time their strong bond steadily bolstered his confidence, and soon the two young cats became devoted friends. When she was out, he then began searching around the hotel seeking its warmest places. Rapidly discovering that Jasper was definitely a sun-worshipper, he can often be observed basking with delight in its rays, following the sun's beams as they move from room to room during the day. The lack of it on dull days was quickly and cleverly resolved: "I have my personal hot hat!" Jasper knowingly says, and nipping onto the desk, with head happily toasting under an anglepoise lamp, looking very curious indeed, yet contented, he blissfully enjoys his warm bonnet.

In time, Jasper displayed he is a wonderful, easy-going and good-natured uncle, endlessly patient with kittens. And, although not fussy about food at all, he did however, once have a very frightening, narrow escape. Returning home one day the woman heard a mysterious, distant, metallic 'clank, clank, clank' sound, which, upon investigation revealed a panicky young Jasper with his head firmly wedged inside an empty salmon tin he'd retrieved from the recycling bin! He suffered no harm, luckily, but this event was sadly prophetic – Jasper's head has proved his weak spot ever since, and its battle-scarred appearance now bears testimony to some nasty bully cats, bad luck, his bravery and fighting technique (or possibly, the lack of it?)

"I like an easy life" he quietly says, "Sunbathing, fun with my friends and caring for kittens, that's all," but in the neighbourhood, patrolling the walls around the hotel gardens, some big, very mean cats regularly prowled, and they thought quite differently.

Never a cat to look for trouble and the gentlest of cats indoors, Jasper has often been challenged outside by many rougher cats. And despite his disposition, whilst still a youngster he seemed to appoint himself as the hotel guardian, ever diligently protective of his patch and instantly alert should any strangers roam this way. "I will look after you all," he heroically says. If you saw his determined defensive stance, you might well think surely an intruder would be sufficiently deterred: his head goes down preparing to butt like a little black bull ready to charge! But never becoming a large cat he was just no match for the big, burly ruffians. Jasper's fearlessness in the face of aggression has resulted in a number of nasty encounters, unfortunately, resulting eventually in a disfigured, yet still dignified head.

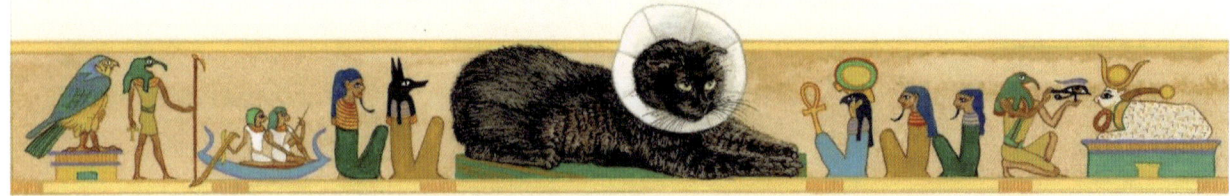

Countless times Jasper's skirmishes have taken him to the vets: "Oh! Jasper! You're back again! Which one's been bullying you this time?" enquired Kim the vet's nurse, and Sheila added with a smile, "Of course we do love to see you, but I really do wish those nasty cats would clear off and leave you alone!"

Numerous wounds have been stitched and bandaged, ointments applied, pills stoically accepted and injections given by the vet, and with quiet dignity, consistently calm and ever-compliant, Jasper never moans. Due to his many injuries and subsequent treatments,

Jasper has ended up having to wear a neck collar a number of times. And unlike any other cat, especially reluctant and grumpy when wearing such an alien encumbrance, with Jasper it is bravely borne with a stately fortitude and never a hint of complaint.

Immediately though, once recovered, the sequence was invariably the same: "Well, now I'm better I ought to check the boundary walls for intruders and tell them who is boss around here!" Unfortunately his gallantry and diligence is always outmatched by the number, sheer size and fighting skills of his powerful opponents.

With his repeatedly frequent trips to see the vet, Jasper became a popular visitor to the surgery, being a rare cat that appears to have total trust in humans. Such a valiant veteran and no stranger to bandages, the model patient has now been affectionately nicknamed 'King Tut' by Kim and Sheila at the vets. It is strange to reflect that amulets of jasper, carved by

the ancient Egyptians with symbols and inscriptions, were buried with the mummified remains of people and their cats in the pyramids for safe passage into the afterlife. Worn by shamans, priests and kings, jasper was considered sacred from ancient times, and the name the surgery staff chose perfectly reflects this precious, heroic chum. Many times on collecting him after operations, the woman would be met by a bandaged and collared vision of feline calm: serenely stretched out, paws in front, looking just like the Sphinx from ancient Egypt.

Jasper has had a rather rough time of things with his health. When some front teeth were lost, his torn pink tongue began to pop through and after a time he has also gone blind in one eye. His ears have taken so many blows that one has sadly collapsed resulting in a rather unique appearance, that of a real warrior and one that belies his true peace-loving nature. A face that would frighten kittens, you might assume! Not so: like little magnets they are mesmerised and kindly educated by this venerable sage. Always willing and eager to show young cats the ways of the world, Jasper's patience and enthusiasm are immeasurable.

And should another cat misbehave provoking a human reprimand, Jasper quickly rallies and acts as second-in-command with a swift yet gentle, but firm rebuke, deftly reinforcing the rules!

A chatterbox, most evident when high winds howl, he rushes wildly around the hotel as if chasing it away with his voice. Equally vocal with cats as with people, Jasper has a lot to say about most things! Attracted instantly by the playing of a game of dice, and politely positioning himself on the sidelines, he declares: "You can rely on me to be silent at important times!" There's nothing Jasper likes more than assuming the role of referee. Every shake and tumble is keenly and patiently monitored with just a muted, muttered remark occasionally passed. Unlike certain other hotel residents who dash in with a careless and playful paw, Jasper knows that humans' games are very serious sport.

Leo and Jasper wash and contentedly curl up asleep entwined together, always the closest of friends and a steadfast team. But despite her best efforts Leo has failed to generate any real interest in observing wildlife from Jasper. Secretly the humans are glad and happily relieved if fewer bedraggled offerings are brought home to the hotel by the pals. So you can imagine the shock one day, outside in the grounds – Jasper was running towards the hotel at speed with a blackbird in his mouth! A sharp intake of breath was quickly followed by the woman's loud, incredulous exclamation: 'JASPER!' His typically vocal reply in response was instant,

and suddenly silenced, he stood still, gazing up in wide-eyed, mute confusion, following after the bird as it escaped, soaring swiftly in flight, unharmed, safely back towards the trees in proof of his gentleness. And thankfully, Jasper has shown no further interest since in such pursuits!

Brightly chattering, whilst blissfully kneading and chewing hair till it resembles wet string, there's no cat here more friendly and affectionate. His obvious courage and sunny disposition are evident by his popularity. Some might call him a little bossy now and then, but actually, he says "I am the leader, watching carefully over all of you and protecting the hotel from any unwanted intruders." Clearly Jasper thoroughly enjoys human company and conversation and asks for nothing: well, just a lovely warm place to rest and a delicious secret morsel from time to time.

Reserved Roland
The dreamer with hidden depths

Roland has spent all of his life at the hotel, yet his arrival here was a very remarkable and astonishing event! He is the only kitten born at the hotel that has stayed – and he is one of life's dreamers – most of the time. So, if you are ever passing along this way and see a huge, furry (possibly slightly grumpy-looking) cat lazily sitting in the garden, it may well be Roland.

He was always different! It was originally assumed that because Leo, his mother, was so young, she'd only had two kittens in her first litter: born in the evening, both looked fine and were of a normal kitten-size. Naturally keen next morning to see how the newborns were doing, the humans went straight to the nest, peering in, but were completely astonished and could hardly believe their eyes: there he was: a colossal surprise – an extra and enormous kitten-number-three! He had evidently put in his first appearance some considerable time after his two littermates had already been born, and was larger by far than his siblings, (he actually looked weeks old), and was filling the nest with his long dark fur – Roly Poly!

And although looking as though he might be some way ahead in kitten-development, judging by size, it was actually entirely the opposite case! So happily was Roland ensconced in that warm, snug place, he undoubtedly became reluctant to leave those lovely, lazy days behind. His other two litter-mates were naturally curious about the world outside their safe shelter, but not Roland: "I like it best here", he simply said. He was not keen to try meat like them, or mix with the bigger hotel cats: "I don't want to!" mother's milk was fine by Roly. With long, striped dark fur and handsome face, his delayed progress persuaded the woman that perhaps his big paws would be happier padding around the hotel and being close to his mother. Continually ignoring entreaties from his adventurous black and white brother and his cute, fluffy tabby and white sister to leave and play, pensive Roland was regularly encouraged, but not persuaded.

However, Leo is a very bright, active cat and her evident impatience with her young duffer's delayed independence began to slowly build. Despite repeated attempts to cajole her demanding son, he remained in the nest far too long. Eventually, the big day did come for this over-sized tabby to finally venture out of his hideaway, and he was so slow to eat solids and explore the world beyond, it was certainly overdue! Leo's mood of exasperation had already noticeably turned to exhaustion, swiftly followed by intolerance. "I am a busy cat and want to go out to see my friends again!" And now keen to resume her hectic social whirl, a clingy kitten as big and needy as Roland hanging around was clearly cramping her style.

At heart serious Roland is rather a softy, and his awareness of this maternal rejection seems to have stung him into menacing action. An unusual new pattern of behaviour then seemed to emerge showing that Roland was not at all soft: 'Roly Poly pudding and pie, chase his Mum and

make her cry' became the hotel's version of the old nursery rhyme and was the rueful comment often heard. His placid expression could change in a flash!

Timed to perverse perfection, Roland's vengeful eyes at first narrow then menacingly glint, and, once Leo's attention has been fully gained: "Called me soft did you? Said I was slow?" they then rapidly shift to a scowling, owl-like glare.

Alarmed, his mother instantly freezes, then in a heartbeat (which allows for her to ineffectually growl), and swiftly galvanised into action, Leo hastily runs, wildly leaping to the highest possible retreat well above the head of her belligerent big bully boy. It appears for Roland, his fun is totally derived in the mischievous 'menace mother' tactic, and the teasing threat and subsequent chase, because no physical attack ever takes place, much to the humans' relief. "Not so slow that time, was I?!" shrewdly retorts ratty Roland.

Often the woman wondered whether Leo has bad and painful memories linked to his delivery: she was only young, a slender cat aged about nine months, and from the start Roland looked several weeks old. Perhaps she has buried resentment in recollection of this traumatic event which is being re-lived every time she looks at him?

Roland's first tentative steps were at last taken into the big world outside the hotel, and that same day something amazing happened! As he toddled cautiously along the path, an uncertain, podgy but handsome bundle of tabby fluff, a cat was watching him intently from a nearby vantage point. With eyes very like Roland's and a body just like an adult version of Roland, he was the most magnificent feline specimen.

Quietly he sat observing the young kitten's progress with great interest. This stranger, who appeared so like Roland, had never been noticed around in the hotel grounds before, but with such a marked resemblance, it was assumed he must be his father. Curiously, this grand cat had perfectly timed his visit to apparently satisfy himself of Roland's existence and was only ever seen on just this one occasion.

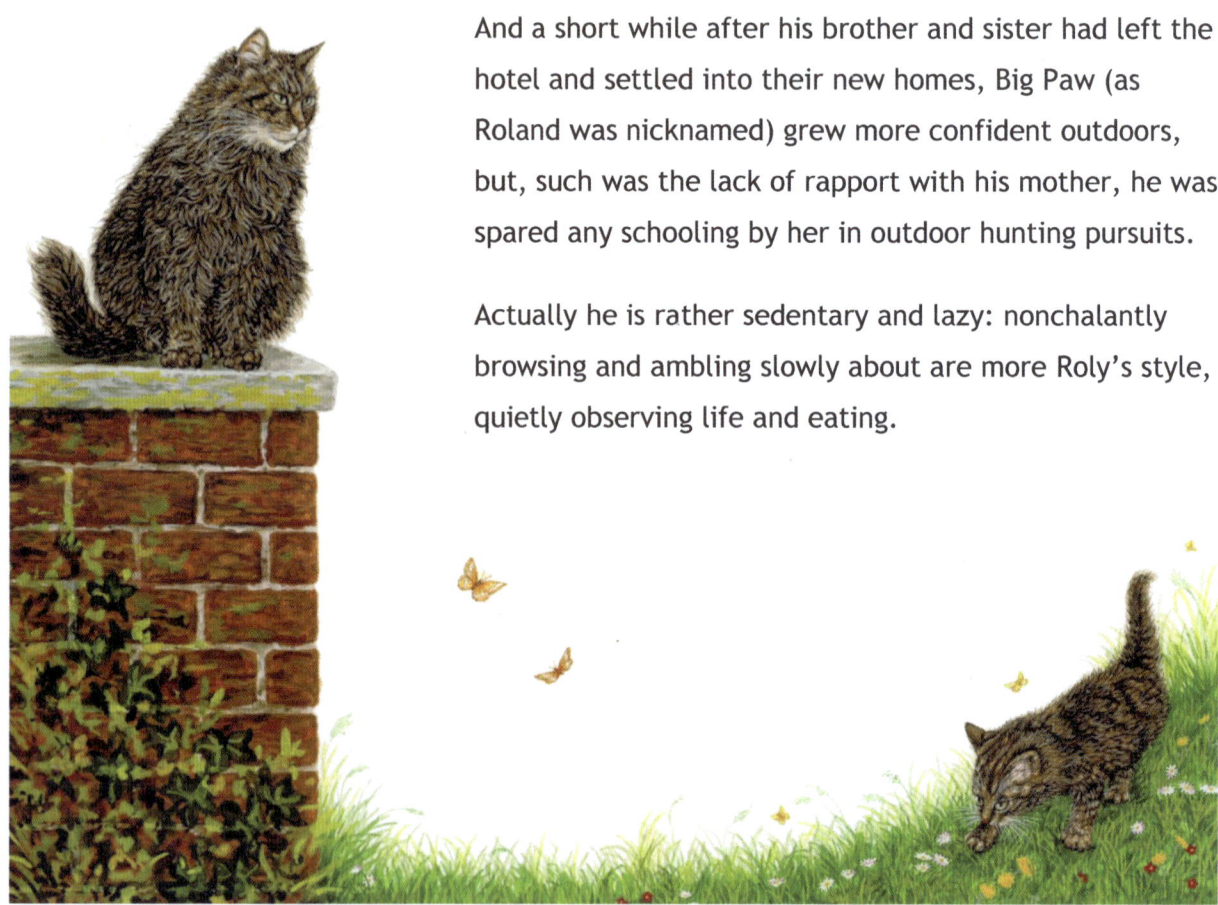

And a short while after his brother and sister had left the hotel and settled into their new homes, Big Paw (as Roland was nicknamed) grew more confident outdoors, but, such was the lack of rapport with his mother, he was spared any schooling by her in outdoor hunting pursuits.

Actually he is rather sedentary and lazy: nonchalantly browsing and ambling slowly about are more Roly's style, quietly observing life and eating.

But the bullies still lurked on the hotel perimeter and a few, rough passing tom cats had other ideas entirely about his quiet life, it was soon discovered. Recurrent squabbles arose as they harangued and assailed his rather hedonistic existence. "Hello wimp! Dreaming again? You're all fur with no fight!" They all seemed to know that despite his great size he was a pushover, a placid, peace-loving cat. As Roland grew into an adult his striking face was framed by a splendid, impressive ruff. Unfortunately, when out in the grounds, confrontations frequently arose, and with every single clash, his neck took the brunt of the aggressors' claws. Regrettably abscesses would form in the same places, and his neck was regularly sore and swollen. Definitely not a natural-born fighter, Roland may look large and fit to challenge any adversary, but he always suffers most in any fracas. "They picked on me again!" his crestfallen face said it all, as unluckily, he became a repeated and unwilling visitor to the vet's surgery.

After a while his marvellous ruff became tatty and sadly depleted, and the skin on his neck had suffered so badly his wounds wouldn't heal properly anymore; he was a very sorry sight.

Dispirited, he would mournfully protest as the basket came out with seemingly alarming frequency. "No! I don't want to go there again, I hate the vets: it always hurts!" Unlike Jasper, so compliant, Roland was the most impatient patient, and (like his Mother Leo), one who also clearly has a mind of his own.

Put into the basket yet again, Roland, loudly disgruntled, had this time devised a cunning plan. "I definitely said: I do not want to go back there!" Walking the well-known mile to the vets, the woman with her heavy cargo, noisily protesting, drew even more attention than usual. Then, all of a sudden and without any prior warning, in seconds Roland had evidently mustered up super strength – through, or because of his pain – and having rapidly squeezed himself through the tiniest gap between the lid and the wicker carrier, made an abrupt escape, and quick as a flash, running like the wind, he darted into the big park.

Powerless to prevent him, and, dashing, desperately shocked and panicky after him, holding the empty carrier, the woman, completely unable to comprehend what had happened, continuously shouted "Roland, Roland!" but, he was nowhere to be seen. It seemed impossible, but he had totally vanished, and worryingly, with a large, gaping open wound in his neck. Although, curiously, as cats often do, canny Roland knew best! The skin on his neck really couldn't take any more stitches, they just wouldn't hold, and this was his extreme and very firm protest.

Worried sick and hoarse with calling, the woman scoured the park's acres feeling more and more hopeless, before eventually returning dejectedly several futile hours later to the hotel, alone. Out came the photos and with the ominous word: 'MISSING', written in large, bold letters, the notices were quickly distributed and displayed. The rest of the long, distracted day the same frantic call was heard all around: "Roland!" repeated with steadily mounting concern. Big Paw was so fond of home life – and in his illness and distress, urgently in need of medical care, all alone in the big, wide park some little distance from the hotel with its many trees, hills and lakes, or wherever he may have wandered. When it turned dark, deepening anxiety suddenly changed instantly to relief, as a very familiar "Miaow" was heard – there he was: tired, hungry and with dead leaves stuck to his open wound.

Recounting Roland's trials at the surgery the next day, with one miserable, still-protesting cat, the vet reappraised the situation. From that morning he said, there was now a fantastic new cream and Roland was going to be the first cat in town to try it! And thankfully, it worked like magic and in no time at all he seemed so much happier, his neck was healing up, and the poor reluctant fighter was evidently in less pain. His glorious ruff has never quite recovered its luxuriant fullness, but thankfully Roly has adopted a less adventurous, cautious, cushion-and-fireside existence, made all the more complete by the presence of another recently arrived hotel resident, Tufty: but you can read more about that love match later...

Really, naturally rather indolent, Roland's energies are now more focussed towards gastronomic appreciation. Fond of titbits and adept at begging, "There must surely be a taste for me!" he sits on his back legs like a furry megalith drooling for cheese or fish or prawns or any other dainty morsel that might tickle his refined taste buds. And – woe betide a refusal or denial! "I can frown, and my big, deft paws have mastered that fridge door!" How many times have humans returned and been greeted by the gnawed remains of illicitly enjoyed delicacies, whilst being slyly watched by an inscrutable face whose busy tongue always gives the game away?!

Not only possessing a cultured palate but also a cultured ear, the human singing voice entrances Roland: happily purring, completely enraptured in his appreciation, he will loudly demand more and more: "Please! Sing me that song again!" Evidently sometimes fatigued by the rigours of gazing into flames and lounging for endless, long hours, yet if bubbles are being blown for him Roland sparkles with delight, captured by their shiny, ephemeral mystery. At heart this large, sometimes-sophisticated cat is really a loveable little kitten!

Passionately keen on the hairbrush, he will drool deliriously and stand up on his back legs to kindly assist with optimum grooming. "I do like to look my very best!" This cooperation is fortunate because his curly sheepskin stomach fur and long, thick tail benefit greatly from regular attention. "Yes!" the woman often says after a session: "It's true! You are just so extraordinarily handsome!"

Although on one occasion, she was casually telling a friend (perhaps rather insensitively) that Roland is a lovely, lazy, adorable lump, who hadn't inherited Leo's prowess in hunting skills – a comment that he evidently heard, and irritated, directed an unmistakably icy glare at the woman. Then, with a sudden vertical jump, Roland leapt from the cosy cushion where he had been quietly snoozing, and with a frosty frown, bearing a distinctly offended air, stalked huffily off. To the humans' horror, within the hour they saw Roland posted sentinel on the landing, and a damp frog was sitting, dripping between his paws. Astonished, and rapidly scooping up the dazed amphibian, the woman offered profuse apologies to Roland as well as the slimy victim of her seemingly careless words. Then the poor frog was swiftly returned to the garden pond, unharmed.

Now in the hotel it is generally understood: the humans realise Roland's contemplative lifestyle has been adopted entirely from choice: meditation, not wildlife-molestation, holds more appeal for this subtly cerebral individual. He has obviously inherited Leo's considerable and canny brain, including the ability to hunt (which he reluctantly only exercised the once, thankfully), but he has chosen another – much more zen – way of life! Roland has taught us a very valuable lesson: NEVER underestimate and always RESPECT YOUR CAT!

Melancholy Marley
The most marvellous mother

Marley is the Cheshire Cat without the grin who always walks alone and sleeps alone. A robust tortoiseshell with an unmistakable air of melancholy, her sturdy frame belies a troubled mind.

The woman heard wailing outside one evening and the hotel echoed to a plaintive, strange, loud cry "Meeeoowaar!" Opening the door to investigate, an unknown, small cat ran determinedly inside. It was a nervous kitten, barely a year old, and when spoken to softly, she replied again once more with an emphatic "Miaaaaoow!" Realising she seemed desperately hungry she was quickly given something to eat. Devouring it instantly, she didn't pause, and dashing straight back to the door, rapidly disappeared.

At around the same time the following evening, back she came, bearing a gift this time: a large piece of chicken skin. Still she had the same insistent sad song and agitated presence – "Meeeeeeooooooooooooowww!" and after an urgently consumed meal, she promptly vanished again. Her loud wailing made the woman think of Bob Marley's group 'The Wailers', and she began to call her Marley, which somehow seemed to readily suit her.

Mournful miaowing once more heralded Marley's return on the third day, and surprisingly she arrived with several bacon rinds! How did she do it? Where on earth was this clever little cat finding these treasures? Quick was the word: a quick cry, "meeooowww", a quick feed, and off she would hurriedly go again.

Weighed down with a ham bone the fourth evening Marley duly arrived, and although ravenously hungry, her (rather grubby) gift was dragged in and placed on the kitchen floor, and the hotel's welcome offering was once more rapidly and eagerly gobbled down.

The following day (a Monday), she brought in the remains of someone's roast joint; and just what that someone thought at its disappearance the woman could only speculate! As always Marley only paused to cry, "mmeeeow!" rapidly gulp down whatever was put on the plate, and just as swiftly dash off.

On the sixth day the woman was bestowed with a gift of raw, fatty meat trimmings, they were no sooner delivered then, after another meal hastily eaten, as usual she urgently left the hotel.

Although encouraged and welcome to stay after eating her food, jittery Marley could not be persuaded, and demonstrating an unmistakable pressing need, with another pleading "Miaoooow!" she would rapidly depart. By now, thoroughly puzzled with visions of this plaintive little wailer surreptitiously raiding neighbours' kitchens and bins, it was assumed by the humans there was something about her they didn't know – and they were absolutely right!

On the seventh day at dusk her loud crying announced as before that she had arrived, and the door was opened – and in she quickly came, closely followed by three tabby kittens! This was her clever plan! Naturally the woman tried to make them immediately welcome but was amazed to discover they were completely wild! Round and round they ran, harum-scarum throughout the hotel, hiding, peeping and hissing, and all the time being offered reassurance by what must have been an exhausted mother! She had obviously worked overtime to find all the gifts she'd brought as well as look after her young, and, filled with admiration the humans were greatly impressed.

The kittens were completely unused to life indoors, and Marley appeared to be somehow traumatised: introverted, unsure, she was very different to all the other cats and completely kept her distance. Observing Marley, there seemed to be elements of a wildcat in her looks: the thick tail, the very dense coat, the round head, solid, muscular body and particular markings. Surely she wasn't wild herself if she was able to trust the woman instantly, as she had so many times, with unwavering certainty? Still her wail could regularly be heard

"Meeooow!" even though she mainly chose to lead a low-profile away from the cat-crowd existence, tucked unobtrusively in a cupboard. Her priority was her litter and she focussed almost entirely on them. Two of the kittens were female and they thankfully quietened noticeably within a few weeks, but the little male was not quite so easily calmed. At the stage when solid food was being discussed and considered for the youngsters, Marley must have thought the time was right too. In she walked with a whole live mouse, a special motherly gift for little Tom. Without hesitation he greedily gulped it down, its tail wriggling on its fateful last journey.

Suitable homes were found for all of them, and by this time the two female kittens were very happily domesticated, lovely and friendly and ready to start their new lives.

But little Tom was last to go, and he remained a rather uncertain quantity. A mother and her young son had enthusiastically phoned and arranged to give him a home and, excitedly, basket in hand, they arrived to collect him. As he raced wildly at high-speed around the hotel, they watched wide-eyed, heads rotating in unison as they followed him in open-mouthed amazement. Obviously feeling up to the challenge, and not expressing any trepidation, his new people patiently waited until he could at last be caught.

It was clear life had been hard for Marley but at

this stage not knowing her background story the woman could only wonder. She was friendly and trusting with her, almost all of the time. But, although she clearly wanted stroking, every so often mid-stroke the purring would suddenly stop and wild-eyed, she'd grab the hand that stroked in a vice-like hold, and using the pressure of her sharp claws and teeth, leave the woman frozen, unable to move at all. It became a nervous, painful waiting game. With visions of blood and in fear of a sudden, savage attack, the woman, tense and wincing, whilst speaking kind words of reassurance, waited until eventually the iron grip released, the savage wildness in her eyes subsided, and the claws retracted. There was certainly much unpredictability about this mysterious cat: she had surely been damaged by an event or memory. Marley has taken a long time and a lot of love for this behaviour to subside, but over time it has greatly diminished, thankfully.

Marley had definitely been food-deprived and used to eat rapidly and voraciously, and she was greedily ready to forcibly tuck into the next cat's share too, so a careful eye had to be kept on her at mealtimes. "Oi!" said the other cats, frequently, protesting: "It's mine!" and monitoring was required for some time. She has adjusted and slowed down now, eventually understanding that there's always another meal at the hotel, but it has been quite a long process.

Marley was such a good mother it was decided that perhaps the best thing, and a potentially positive, calming influence, would be if she was allowed to have another litter in the hotel without all the stress she'd suffered before. Keeping a low profile and understanding, when the time came she obligingly used the prepared, snug, secure nest for her kittens, but as soon as they were delivered, one by one she proudly picked them up, carried them straight to the woman and put them on her knee! Very honoured and surprised, stroking the appreciative cat, she exclaimed, "You are amazing Marley! Very well done!" and regularly making sure she was happy, well fed and looked after, the young mother continued to quietly bring up her litter.

Curiously, the truth about her past was subsequently revealed when the people arrived to take Marley's last kitten from her second litter to his new home: they instantly recognised her. Apparently, they related, she originally lived in a large nearby house which was divided into flats. There had been trouble there with some very unpleasant and crazy people and this eventually culminated in a house fire. Marley, they said, had carried her tiny new-born kittens to the safety of a nearby churchyard where she had stayed for weeks caring for them alone, before she came to the hotel. It was a safe and sheltered, private spot, an old church with overgrown grounds at the back, very near to the hotel and a perfect choice to give her tiny kittens protection and peace. This young cat with superb mothering skills must have then secretly observed the hotel and its residents, and, satisfied, instinctively known she would be safe there and made welcome. The woman was pleased and relieved Marley could now live in a caring environment without any distress after hearing of the trauma and hardship she'd previously experienced.

Marley has settled well, although still refuses to mix or relax with other cats, preferring her own or the woman's company. Beds and hidey-holes in cupboards are her favourite: she looks for the safest, quietest, most secluded nooks, inconspicuously tucked away. Generally reclusive and keeping a low profile, contact with other cats is just occasionally made, and usually then only if they are sleeping in a fancied, warmed place she can poach. She will perform a perfunctory few licks to the sleeping cat's head, and then promptly evict the poor creature, claiming its cosy bed as her due.

No one messes with Marley! The claws are always ready, and the sad, wild eyes warn strongly against this.

Very often she has a faraway look and a lost, sorrowful stare, but now the mournful voice no longer exists. Returning to the hotel one day after a routine operation, she opened her mouth, and the only noise that emerged was a squeak like a rusty hinge! Her voice had vanished at the vets!

Continually alert and super-swift outdoors, Marley runs and expertly scales up trees as if they are part of the horizontal plane!

And perhaps on one occasion she was too curious, because she now has a new, distinctive round mark on the centre of her lovely orange nose, probably the result of a sting, where the fur has never grown back.

There's more than a little of the wildcat about Marley. The merest whiff of raw food shows instant evidence of this, and scraps are always fed in a cautious and judicious manner, and at a sensible distance, so as to avoid certain injury!

Marley had a very sad early life but triumphed against the odds; she demonstrated clearly she is a most marvellous, intelligent mother who thankfully, has mellowed considerably over time. Now safe, happier and well-fed: in her very calmest moments quite often these days there's a glimpse of the Cheshire Cat, still without a grin, but at least sometimes with the hint of a little smile.

Nifty Tufty
Mistress of subtle surprise

Loveable Tufty! She came – she saw and she quickly conquered hearts. One glimpse through the hotel window was all she needed to see: "I know I would like one of those chairs very much!" or, she thought: "possibly a soft, woolly lined basket might be better?" Then, she decided: "That rug in front of the fire looks the best of all, and there is something I particularly like about the big, dark, striped cat who is lying there; is he the most handsome? Yes – I really do think so!"

The hours went by and her pitiful vocal request for admission never ceased. Peering intently through the window, Tufty absolutely knew – there was no doubt: this was all she could ever wish for. "But we are getting very full here at the hotel you know, we mustn't rock the boat too much", said the woman to another human, "Do you think she might already have a home somewhere else?" "NO! I haven't" said the rather-too-slim cat determinedly, "I was abandoned, and, by the way, I am also extremely hungry too!"

The evening approached, yet the observant little face was still pressed persistently to the glass, and rooted to the ledge, she gazed enviously through the window, watching, patiently waiting, sadly crying, whilst the fat cats lazed and lounged and sauntered occasionally to plates laden with all sorts of delicious-looking things. "Miaoooow! I'm still here, I am positive this is the right place, and I definitely won't go!"

Suddenly the door was at last flung open: "Come on then!" was the laughing invitation and, in a short, magical second, little Tufty gleefully skipped inside. Straight away the woman said "Oh, look! One of her back feet is just pink and has no claws, and she only has a little tail! I wonder: has she had an accident? She must be at least four and whatever happened to her, it wasn't recently; just notice how nimble she is!"

After a very long time without a proper meal, and certainly not one eaten off a plate, Tufty was soon served something wonderfully tasty and after eating, appreciatively, she felt much better. Then immediately Roland saw Tufty's bright, pretty eyes, he knew as well: it was love at first sight! And smoothly fitting in, as though she'd always been part of the gang, her calm rapport with all the other cats was the best outcome imaginable, and blissfully happy, united with Roland, their special, firm friendship grew.

Despite her disability which causes her to limp badly, Tufty has developed a nimble and swift three-legged run. With her beautiful face and steady gaze, it was soon discovered she possesses an enchanting, irresistible, magnetic nature. Just before she arrived, some old houses had been demolished nearby and the humans wondered: could she have been left behind or become lost when someone had moved?

Initially jittery and rather nervous, she did show obvious signs of neglect and was rather thin: how long had Tufty wandered hungry and homeless before finding the Cats' Hotel? All that rapidly changed with Roland as her handsome champion, and soon she became much calmer and more confident. Resting, enjoying good food and care, as well as the company of the other cats, charming Tufty blossomed beautifully, and her coat and condition noticeably improved.

"I just love it here: when I want to, I can sit on a warm knee again, just like I used to!" Tufty, purring, loving and very friendly, made it clear, she had lived in a home once before. "I wonder what her background was and whether she ever had kittens?" the woman mused, although there was no sign of a maternal streak showing in Tufty – yet! Then one memorable day, a friend visited, an elderly lady called Elizabeth, accompanied by her old and well-behaved poodle, Shandy, and the humans thought again. Chatting outside in the garden, as was usual (so the dog did not upset any nervous hotel residents), the woman and Elizabeth quietly stood, in conversation, innocently enough. Tufty's sharp eyes had spotted this seemingly suspicious, regular canine caller for the first time though, and, in a flash, like a Kung Fu Master she leapt, in an unexpected attack, pouncing on the poor little pooch. Yelping in shock, Shandy's fur flew, and as she sank in her claws the old dog shrieked in pain, and swiftly both the shaken owner and stunned poodle made a hasty retreat, which was clearly in the pair's best interest!

Straight afterwards and back indoors, quite deliberately, Tufty made an uncustomary bee line directly towards Marley's litter lying in their nest, totally oblivious to the fuss. Gently she picked up one of the kittens and then protectively carried it away. With great care and tangible curiosity, she tended to it at a little distance as if instinctively sampling (or maybe remembering?) the role of 'Mum'.

Watching squirrels and birds from the warmth of a window-ledge inside the hotel always amuses and entertains Tufty for hours, and induces the woman's laughter as Tufty's teeth chatter like castanets. "I am concentrating, mustn't lose my touch, but I do hope the necessity will never arise again!"

Clearly Tufty had hunted in order to eat as a homeless cat; now, although there is no longer that need, she still eagerly watches the wildlife. On one occasion in the garden, her enthusiastic, habitual observation provoked the wrath of a mother blackbird and, after approaching too closely, she was repeatedly dive-bombed in warning until she scuttled safely back indoors.

Never slow to miss an unguarded moment of opportunity at meal times, any tasty items reposing upon a human's plate will be swiftly removed by sleight of Tufty's paw and reallocated. A deeply ingrained opportunistic survival streak was not so easy for her to forget: but a little charmer who has often gone hungry surely can't be blamed, can they? An appetising piece of fresh fish or perhaps a nicely grilled kipper does require especial vigilance on the human's part. "I couldn't help myself! I completely forgot. I am sorry. Errr, would you like it back?" But the woman is never cross with Tufty, it seems impossible: something about her beguiles and always instantly evokes joy. "No, thank you Tufty, though I do think I was terribly careless!"

When humans leave the hotel to go out, there is usually a black and white furry sentry who now posts herself at the gate, but she has an ulterior

motive, and peeping from amongst shrubs, ever-watchful, she is ready to say a relaxed "Goodbye!" This bright mistress of subtle subterfuge has secret plans, though: silently, stealthily, she will often go too! Five minutes into the journey an  alert, familiar face regularly suddenly pops up over the wall! "I came too – surprise rendezvous!" Obviously her past experience has lent this feline a superb A-Z knowledge of every road and lane and wall and garden and nook and cranny within quite an extensive radius of the hotel!

One day the woman's mother had visited the hotel and she left to walk a mile or two back to her home with a wicker shopping basket on wheels. Some considerable distance away she stopped, briefly pausing, and guess whose lovely little face popped up out of her trolley?! "I thought I'd come along and meet your cats for a change, just to say hello!"

And that quiet, summer-evening drink the humans sometimes planned at the pub ten minutes walk away? Often they are forced to abandon their plans and forget it – it's very likely a sudden furry ambush will mean they are forced to! Who could relax with an adventurous Tufty wandering fearlessly about, casually mingling amongst groups of people and keenly greeting arriving cars as they park? "It's OK! Please let's all stay a while! I like it here" is always Tufty's calm response to the woman's agitation: "I used to come sometimes and ask for snacks and clean up bits off the paving in the beer garden you know!"

This cat will gently tap humans awake with her dainty paw and wash their faces to make sure they get up when she is ready, but ironically she is the reason they are sometimes late! If not taken back and regularly returned safely home, it is feared even the intrepid Tufty might at some time get lost. And who knows? Perhaps that is what happened when she became homeless; although later the humans heard another possible story……..

Some might say she is disabled, although it seems never to have stopped her in any way. Despite her limp, purposeful Tufty still moves faster by far than several of the rather indolent residents (who shall remain nameless), and is decidedly a great deal more adventurous.

After Tufty had been at the hotel for a while, a friend called to visit, and he offered a possible explanation for her foot with no claws and short tail. Years before he had worked in a large paper mill miles away on the edge of the town, and he went on to explain that many cats were born there in inaccessible places, some very high up behind pipes and big machinery, and all of them were black and white. Often, because of inbreeding amongst the cats of the factory colony, he remembered kittens that were born with deformities, and he thought little Tufty looked like one of these cats and conjectured she might have originally been brought, or potentially have travelled from there.

Tufty certainly has her own distinctive, very individual traits, and revealed she does prefer her own private drinking well – the paw prints around the toilet bowl are constant proof of this: "Somehow it is much more refreshing than the water in the communal cats' bowl!" she firmly says.

Once as the woman was watching her gulping happily away, her delicate balance on the shiny rim was lost, and splash! Tufty had an unplanned quick dip in her personal porcelain well! Gregarious Tufty loves to energetically travel around, mingle with people and cats and enthusiastically explore new places. Yet, she is so totally in her element when curled up with Roland: they will peacefully lounge for long, contented hours by bright flames, purring, toasting, lovingly warm together.

This beautiful much-loved hotel cat has not only found her own perfect home, but her very best friend was waiting here for her too!

Tenacious Tuppence
The cat who was left behind

The house had no curtains and the windows never lit up anymore: even the doorway had cobwebs across it, it had been empty so long, yet the sad little cat still sat forlornly hugging the lonely step. Tuppence was dreaming again: she heard Rachel humming and imagined hopefully she'd be bringing something tasty for her tea, but, opening her eyes, dismayed, saw a different girl pass by. "Even a taste of Oliver's pizza would be better than nothing I'm sure" Tuppence mused, although after waiting so long she couldn't quite recall how pizza tasted anymore, or exactly how Oliver looked. "In the beginning when Duncan and Rosie lived here too, it was much better: they nearly always remembered to bring me something home, even if sometimes it was just cat biscuits. I'd love a big bowl of them now, though that was when I was having my kittens, so that was a long while ago".

The students had been gone for many months, and the doors of the vacant house had been locked when they left. No one came any more. Wearily Tuppence started her rounds, "Maybe the old man at the corner cottage has had bacon today and perhaps he's saved me the rinds!" Sitting patiently at his back door, it stayed closed too: he was out.

"I wonder if the children at No. 10 might give me a few of their cat's biscuits?" she hoped, listening, but again, it was quiet. The only sounds she heard were the ravenous rumblings inside her, and they drove her farther along the old lane, but after a few other futile attempts to find something to eat, she still had no result. Resigned, Tuppence slowly, dejectedly, went back to where she had started, by the step of the deserted house where no one but her could be seen.

In a fitful sleep under a damp bush, early the next morning she was woken very suddenly by the noise of a nearby vehicle and voices, and they all sounded new and strange. Blinking awake, Tuppence saw baskets being placed by her door, and in every one an unfamiliar, grumpy-looking cat was sitting, and most had quite a lot to say. "They are going into my home!" Tuppence observed, amazed, and quietly sitting unobtrusively where she thought no one could see her, she peeped cautiously from a corner of the garden.

It wasn't long before a woman who came with the cats, was speaking to a lady who lived across the lane, and they were talking about her. "They just left her when they finished studying; she sneaked into the neighbour's bedroom next door and had a litter of kittens on their bed, but they threw her out. She then brought them up somewhere outside in thick snow, terrible, and still only so young herself; we occasionally give her scraps, but she won't leave that house. They called her Tuppence".

Soon after, she again heard her name, and saw the same new woman approaching with a plate of very delicious-smelling food, "Hello Tuppence! Do you want to come inside?" was her friendly entreaty. "I'd rather not" was the solemn cat's instant, flat reply, but, she swiftly added, "I do feel extremely hungry though, so thank you for the lovely meal", and heartily she polished off every single speck until the plate positively shone.

"How are you Tuppence? Will you come in today?" the woman cheerfully enquired the following morning as she placed another delightfully full dish on the ground. "Have you changed your mind yet?" But having only ever lived as a solo cat before, the shock of seeing a throng of strangers, interlopers in her home, made her feel decidedly nervous, and meant the answer again was a definite "No!"

Relishing each marvellous item on the menu, Tuppence began to put on weight, and although still introverted, looked and felt more confident. But although she liked the woman and always enjoyed her company, Tuppence remained unsure about all of the other cats who had arrived with her. Quite soon after though, the woman's firm words were telling her: "I insist! I see you are going to have more kittens, and I want to show you the nicest, safe nest I have made indoors, especially for you!" "Oh no!" said Tuppence warily, "not inside". So the woman, reluctantly understanding, arranged a dry shelter outside, undercover in a brick alcove, using a large old wooden chest, lined with wool blankets, saying "At least the weather is warm!" And Tuppence, approving, was suddenly more settled and began feeling much better again.

There was always tasty food to enjoy, and the woman chatted and frequently fussed and stroked her. And when her three cute kittens were safely born, they were all healthy: the female was a very pretty tortoiseshell, and the two brothers: a gentle, handsome-looking black kitten and a lively black and white one.

The trio grew strongly, and after a few months, the beautiful young female found herself a home down the road, and the sleek black male also worked his charms on another family nearby. Appearing contented with his routine, the black and white kitten stayed on, now and then curiously peeking around the hotel door, but eating his meals outside, and always ready

to go off exploring again: and energetic and active, he appeared totally fascinated with everything. Extremely friendly and sociable (unlike Tuppence), he enthusiastically played games happily for hours with local children, often jumping up high to catch the ball. Their joyful laughter pealed out extra loudly whenever this jolly, popular kitten joined in their games.

One day when pilchards were served as a special treat for Tuppence and her son, unusually, when called, her young son didn't appear. But, within minutes there was a sudden sharp knock at the front door, and a distressed young boy was standing there, white-faced, with the absent kitten in his arms, and the poor little thing was bleeding profusely from his mouth. The flustered boy, in panic proclaimed shakily: "The kitten has been hit by a motorbike!" Immediately the concerned woman placed the shocked, small cat in a basket and rushed along to the vets, and after they had thoroughly examined him, heard that luckily, the only apparent injury they had found was a badly broken jaw. Suddenly the young kitten's carefree life outdoors was exchanged for a cage at the vets, in preparation for surgery the next morning. And when collecting him later the next day after his operation, they explained everything had gone successfully, and, importantly, the woman was given strict instructions to keep him quiet and carefully purée all of his food. Gently placed in the cat basket, he was soon returned to the sanctuary of a quiet room to convalesce at the hotel.

But astonishingly, before his first meal was prepared, the rapidly improving, alert patient eagerly jumped up and started devouring hungrily: the meat wasn't even properly mashed, never mind puréed! He was boldly behaving just like a perfectly fit kitten without a care in the world, and no one could have ever guessed his jaw was broken the day before. Satisfied, he then confidently nestled into a cushion, and looking like the happiest young cat in town, purring and padding, was as bright as a button. He was remarkably contentedly relaxed, and after the shock of the accident and surgery, at long last resting. It struck the woman he looked like a miniature badger with his lovely black and white markings, and, sitting down beside him, she called him 'Brock', and then drank a toast to his future good health.

The woman began noticing Tuppence now seemed a bit lost and sad, suddenly alone again in the garden; perhaps she was missing her little kitten nearly always so close by his mother. Bringing her in and showing her the thoroughly happy patient recovering inside the hotel, she was obviously relieved and pleased to see him again, and occasionally she then began to quietly come and join Brock indoors: "Well, only for a short visit".

Relieved at this change in her behaviour, another was very soon noticed: she had swiftly become pregnant yet again. Determined this time that Tuppence must stay in the (now more familiar) hotel and give birth inside, the decision was also resolved that this

definitely would be her last litter. And although seemingly sometimes glad to have warmth and rest, relations with the other cats had not really improved. Remaining aloof, Tuppence displayed a crotchety intolerance that was mainly directed towards Leo and Marley, an antipathy which both peevishly returned. "It is my house and you are in it!" she crossly said, scowling in their direction, and they retorted emphatically with "No, you are mistaken, because we live here!"

However, when the new kittens appeared to be imminent, a few days before the event, Tuppence was shown a cosy, prepared box in a safe, quiet corner of the hotel, and, explaining it was just for her and the kittens, this time she seemed to be altogether more amenable and compliant. One chill autumn morning a day or two later Tuppence uncharacteristically refused her breakfast, went unobtrusively into the private box, and with relief all round, she later safely delivered a third healthy brood of three.

No one was more curious about the new arrivals than young Brock, who sat gazing into the nest, as if willing the tiny kittens to hurry and grow up and join in his games.

And as soon as their eyes opened, his eager paws would pat them and try to haul them out to play.

He was so impatient, so excited. The instant they eventually began to emerge he was utterly overjoyed, and in true form, Leo, suddenly more cooperative, took some of the maternal burden off Tuppence, washing, teaching and playing tirelessly with the youngsters. Memories of Leo's mothering instincts had, like magic, suddenly mellowed her frosty feelings. Brock's boundless energy with his three brand-new playmates also ensured life for Tuppence this time, was very much easier.

The weeks flew by into months and soon the kittens were all weaned, growing larger, fully trained and ready to go to new homes.

But when there was only one left, a lady called Linda rang: she had recently come back to the area after living in the Far East for some years, and she wanted two kittens. Explaining her family always loved having cats, she related that whilst living abroad they had looked after a lot.

Terribly disappointed on hearing that just one remained, the woman tentatively enquired whether Linda would be able to consider giving Tuppence a new start with her last kitten. Absolutely thrilled by the solution, she thankfully greeted the idea with great enthusiasm.

So, in freshly falling winter snow, the woman set off with mother and kitten, and was eagerly met by a happy and excited family in a lovely, warm house several miles away.

They were all delighted, and the daughter Lucy had decided to call the little kitten Pod, and Tuppence was to be re-named: they thought Pebble was perfect because of the small spot on her nose. After the long, hard times in her young, sad life, Pebble and her kitten Pod had a fresh new beginning, and a loving, bright future together.

Badger Brock
The magical cat with a secret life

"Mmmmm! Very delicious, thank you!" the black and white kitten spoke brightly, appreciatively licked his mouth vigorously, only for a minute, and glancing just briefly at the woman, he then dashed down the path and nimbly headed back to old Bill's garden. He had secretly seen the gardener leaving earlier, getting his tools from the shed and tunefully whistling as he strode off towards his allotment. Brock contentedly settled in his chosen spot and resumed observing Bill's busy pigeon coop, and as usual, was fascinated by the red-eyed birds' preening, and their chattering, cooing conversations.

As if hypnotised, he drifted off into a long, happy dream, only rousing himself at the sudden siren sound of Bill's squeaking old wheelbarrow returning, groaning with tools and produce.

Deftly nipping unseen through the fence, Brock silently approached the edge of the lush, green-fringed pond at number twenty-six. Mesmerised, he watched the glinting goldfish darting in shimmering, synchronised activity in the dark, mysterious rippling wet deep, and they always enthralled him. He didn't think about anything else for hours until he heard shrill young voices and in instant recognition, he was off again.

Dan and Charlotte were his two favourites: he joined in every single game, and they always laughed and often stroked him. "Chase the ball cute kitty!" Charlotte cried out and nothing ever made Brock happier, leaping and running around playing with them. A little later they were called in for their tea and, after another lovely short snooze, Brock ambled along to the Cats' Hotel, and, as soon as the woman saw him his meal was served, which he enthusiastically ate. "Hello" he greeted Tuppence, his mother, also eating outside next to him, but being much less sociable than he, and a cat of few unnecessary words, just replied with her familiar, but reassuring maternal glance.

Hastily Brock trotted off immediately the plate was empty: "Oh! Must dash! Bye for now!" He'd heard Arthur and his sisters' voices echoing from across the lane. They happily let the lively and popular kitten join in their fun and various games, and often the two young girls carried the kitten to their brightly coloured little house in the garden where they pretended he was their baby, called him silly names, and covered him with a blanket. Enjoying their attention and gentle, fussing prattle, no little cat was more relaxed. The youngest, Olivia said "You are the loveliest kitten in the whole world!" and he even fell blissfully asleep tucked up there, dreaming, only waking when it was dusk and the children had gone into their house.

Casually Brock sauntered home: well, he actually lived outside with his mother, and her reticence meant he'd only popped his head inquisitively just inside the door of the Cats' Hotel once or twice (when she wasn't watching). Settling into their warm, dry shelter, he had a thorough long wash, then curled up next to her and contentedly slept another happy starlit night.

The freedom of his unusual life outdoors meant that sometimes Brock saw things other little cats would never see: the rustling, grunting, noisy approach of the foraging hedgehog, the sleek, silent swoop of the mouse-hunting owl, and quite often, the luminous yellow-eyed warning of the hungry fox heading down to old Bill's pigeon coop, slavering, ever-hopeful.

His brother and sister litter-mates had left their special home some months before; they had both gone to live inside houses.

Now Brock had found his own friends and favourite haunts, and, rambling routinely between them, eating at the hotel whenever he was ready, he couldn't have been any happier, until that terrible day.

Dan had kicked the ball so hard it went over the thick, high privet hedge at the edge of their garden and into the lane with little Brock nimbly chasing behind. And that was the last thing the young cat mistily remembered. Dan, instantly alarmed upon hearing a scream, urgently ran to pick him up, then almost in tears, in a shaky voice he was telling the woman at the front door: "He's been hit by a motorbike", and blood was running all over the handsome kitten's furry black and white face.

Suddenly he was put into a carrying cage and almost frozen in shock, hurriedly taken to see the vet. "He will need x-rays and I will let you know the results later" the serious man in a green coat was telling the woman. Feeling very different to his usual bouncy self, and in this strange, new place, the hours swam uncertainly by.

The next day the woman returned to the surgery for him, and the vet told her "incredibly the only injury he has is a broken jaw which we have fixed. However, all of his food will need to be carefully puréed until he is better. Keep him quiet and bring him back tomorrow so I can check him".

The injured kitten was very pleased to see the familiar lane again that he called home, but this time he went through the front door of the Cats' Hotel and was promptly taken to a quiet room where there were lots of comfortable cushions.

The woman started to prepare his meal and in his hunger and enthusiasm he jumped up and instantly started eating it. "Hey! What about my mashing and puréeing it first, little fellow?

Patience! You're not very well, although I don't think anyone would ever know!" Recuperation suited Brock, but only for a while!

Now she always called him Brock and said with his lovely colours he looked like a small badger. Then the woman brought his mother upstairs to see him, and evidently reassured and pleased, Tuppence joyfully licked his head and spoke: "Where have you been? I have really missed you!" and every day afterwards she came to see him, but refused to stay for long.

"I'll be back out there with you soon!" he cheerfully said, and, looking forward to that day, Brock continued to enjoy life indoors.

Getting better and becoming friendly with the other cats in the Cats' Hotel, it was readily noticed Brock often seemed able to puzzle

and outwit the woman. The purring hummock under the bed covers (his newly discovered, favourite secret lair) always gave the game away and often too – "but how did he ever get through that closed door?" the woman pondered, to herself, frowning, and she said to him "You have magical powers I think!"

When the wind stormily blows, and the rain teems heavily down, the Cats' Hotel is full of fair-weather downcast faces: Brock, though, is just as exuberant, eager, as on a summer's day, energetically trotting off, excitedly exploring, and always entirely to his own agenda.

Someone said they believed Brock's mother had originally been brought to the area from a factory a little distance away on the edge of town where there were lots of cats. Perhaps deep in his genes lies the origins of his love of freedom and passion for the great outdoors; a feral feline seems to lurk in his soul.

"Oh, thank you kind, clever Brock!" she always says, resigned, as another bedraggled, but completely whole trophy is presented proudly upon his return.   And growing up lean and agile, although not large in stature, Brock bravely guards and defends his patch.

Moths are apparently a delicious morsel delicately devoured with relish:

"Yum, yes, my special treat!" With sharp, bright eyes and super-swift paw, he is the absolute master of the vertical jump, and a favourite spot of Brock's in summer is lurking beneath buddleia bushes preying on unsuspecting butterflies fluttering and feasting upon the nectar. A real athlete, lithe, perceptive Brock is ever-ready to spring into action: he seems to fear nothing and miss nothing.

After many hours rambling in remote places, exhaustion will drive him home, and often Brock is soaked and noticeably grubby. Dutifully, he is then routinely compelled to patrol the hotel in case anything has changed in his absence. Every room and cat is diligently visited, and his muddy paws distribute footprints liberally wherever he goes, as he thoroughly checks out his home once again. Finally, when the inspection is completed, after a quick feed, Brock will sit swaying and continuously yawning, obviously totally shattered, but somehow seemingly reluctant to admit the fact. Following a perfunctory wash, he will then eventually

snooze, often lying stretched on his back, relaxing, legs in the air and whiskers twitching as he dreams, purring, perhaps re-living his latest adventures.

Delightful and affectionate with a pronounced independent

streak, Brock has shown a distinct reluctance to return to the vets. When the woman appeared with an empty cat basket one day, he instinctively knew it was for him, and adroitly appearing at the top of the stairs, he performed a nifty tripping manoeuvre sending the woman tumbling and crashing into the hall below.   As she limped in, back from the hospital (some considerable while later), he dashed impatiently to greet her. "You are psychic and also very naughty!" she told him, but, with the morning's protest long-forgotten, he now had more pressing concerns: "Err, will dinner be ready soon, do you think?" Brock responded engagingly: "It is very late tonight".

This cat puts his own twist on all of the rules. Most cats don't like water – but Brock is truly fascinated! Entirely transfixed by a dripping tap he will sit in the bath mesmerised by its slow plip-plop, plip-plop!

With a rare and superior intelligence, Brock has perfected the art of balancing strategically, and, ingeniously, by placing four feet carefully, he will use the humans' toilet for its intended purpose! Absolutely intrigued, he then gazes wide-eyed into the bowl, and is quite mystified at the whoosh of the rushing waterfall when it is subsequently flushed!

The woman was relaxing in the bath one evening, and splash – startled, she jumped, as blithely, Brock had decided to join her with a single agile, springing leap!

Very friendly with Leo and sharing similar interests in local wildlife-watching, Brock will compatibly, contentedly curl up with her and sleep.

But when she wants to join him on his exploits in the garden or further afield, Brock is adamant and makes it quite clear, he is a private individual who prefers to hunt and forage alone.

And Brock must still think he's the size of a kitten because he often seems

determined to squeeze into tiny boxes and kitten-beds intended for much smaller cats.

Woody is his very special pal, and quite regularly they will climb into a big wicker basket and snuggle up in the cushioned woolly depths slumbering together: that is if Brock hasn't first managed to surreptitiously sneak off solo into an out-of-bounds human's bed!

Christmas time brings out the mischief in both Woody and Brock, and inside the hotel they make a naughty, brotherly team.

Brock has always excelled at football and has passed on these skills to his pal. The shiny baubles are adeptly removed from the tree, and the frisky pair will then charge about madly, just interrupting play occasionally to have a wild spree tearing and shredding the fancy paper off gifts arranged at its base.

The night before Christmas usually sees the humans hastily re-wrapping presents and doing their best to locate lost baubles, then hastily re-decorating the tree!

Brock was born outside, and he is equally a bright, friendly charmer and beautiful, cushion-loving cat as much as a free spirit, who with a quick, purposeful run, swiftly vanishes for many hours into the wild shadows to enjoy his secret, solitary adventures.

Wonderful Woody
The tiny kitten who grew and grew

Sneezing and shivering helplessly as February snow began to fall, the sick little kitten's head was spinning: through his running eyes he saw yet another bus whoosh wetly past, and everyone rushed along without noticing the tiny desperate cat; he had waited and waited and waited, and now he could hardly breathe.

Then, suddenly, a pair of hands gently grabbed him, and extremely ill as he was, he thought "This feels so lovely". He heard the woman's voice calling to someone across the road: "Is he yours?" and the brusque reply: "No. Take him – he's been hanging around here for days". To be tucked inside a cosy quilted coat was the best feeling he'd ever known, and after a snuffly twenty minutes snuggled happily there, soon he was sitting on a table in a bright room where a concerned man in a green coat carefully examined the ailing kitten. After looking first at him very seriously, the vet was telling the woman: "He has pneumonia, cat flu and an ear infection. I am sorry, but he is so weak things really don't look too good. I will do all I can: make sure you keep him warm and if he gets through the night, bring him to the surgery again early tomorrow".

"Your fur reminds me of wood smoke, you sad, beautiful kitten, so I will call you Woody" she emphatically said, and together Woody and the woman went swiftly towards the hotel. Then, taken into a room, he was carefully placed on a warm, soft bed, with a hot water bottle, given a little bowl of delicious food, and she whispered to him: "Please grow up big and strong little Woody, and you can live in the Cats' Hotel" and exhausted, he promptly drifted off to sleep: very ill indeed, but snug and happy.

The next day, nestled carefully within woollen blankets inside a carrier cage, they went again to see the man in the green coat, and this time the vet smiled, and Woody thought "I feel a bit better than yesterday". More pills and injections followed the day after, and Woody declared quite certain: "I am a bit stronger again".

Little Woody lay in his peaceful sanctuary back at the Cats' Hotel and now he began to notice there were toys around, and the woman often popped in to see him for a friendly chat: "I like it here and I am much fitter today", Woody cheerfully remarked.

It was lovely to be able to rest and eat good food. Every day he was tucked into the sheltered layers in his basket and went to see the man in the green coat, and every time the vet instantly smiled a little bit wider. And calmly ready on the vet's table for his (by now) routine injections and pills, Woody acquiescently sat on his bottom like a teddy bear, purring in his quiet, trusting way, which over the months that followed, never faltered.

One day at the surgery Woody suddenly noticed something. With each visit whilst in the waiting room, he was hearing a lot about a cat: "Beautiful!", "So handsome!", "Just gorgeous", "Wonderful!", "I'm usually a 'dog person' but he is a special cat!" – and with a very strange feeling, he realised, they were talking about him!

As the weather warmed, Woody's weight increased and he no longer sneezed and snuffled. And stroking his handsome head and smiling broadly, the vet, pleased with his progress, decided he could now safely schedule future visits on alternate days. Thankfully Woody was getting well, and although still isolated in his hotel sick bay he contentedly rested, and with newly found energy began to play enthusiastically with his toys. Special fun structures were created for him out of cardboard boxes joined together making tunnels and hidey holes through which he wildly ran chasing catnip mice and balls. And demonstrating he is extremely affectionate, Woody always loved the woman's company and attention: everything had gradually become a source of fun.

Back at the hotel he was still alone in his lovely, private recovery room although now he was feeling fine, much more settled, and growing bigger and healthier each day.

For some weeks Woody had been aware that he wasn't the only cat who lived in the Cats' Hotel. Although murmurs had previously been softly whispered in polite recognition, now he had almost fully recuperated he decided, "Today I will properly introduce myself", and sounding eerily like a mermaid perched on a rock in the ocean, the high-pitched, unearthly performance began. Spellbound, and thoroughly impressed, the cats on the other side of the wooden door silently listened, mutually entranced by his soulful song. Over the following weeks, Woody frequently began singing: serenading the others with his hauntingly original melodies and now he thought: "I love my cardboard tunnels, and I like playing ball, but even more I wish I could meet new friends!" and then, suddenly, the door to his room opened.

"Now you're well Woody, come and meet your new friends" she said.

And it was true: they all loved him straight away: cool and composed, he quietly sat side by side with the older residents, sharing peaceful, meditative moments. He even mixed a little with the shy ones,

the woman calling him "A miracle worker" who seemed to have achieved the impossible by charming Marley, the loner.

And, in a short while sociable Woody was allowed to explore outside. Then his adventures with young Brock began: his new, favourite best friend for fun and many mischievous games.

The warm days suited him nicely, and thoroughly enjoying lots of lovely food and treats he grew even bigger. Unfortunately, Woody started to rather fancy the human's food as well:

"Please, just a little piece of buttered toast", or, he implored, gazing with beautiful eyes beseechingly "can you spare a small taste of Cheddar cheese?", "perhaps one crunchy potato crisp?"

His ultimate carbohydrate delight was soon discovered: a freshly baked loaf! Scattered slices littered the hallway, each one sampled and approved, and when the woman came home she exclaimed: "Oh! Woody! Silly me! Did I leave the loaf out again? This won't help your waistline will it? I know you were hungry when you came here, but the vet has noticed lately – you are getting a little bit F-A-T!"

Woody, outside for long, exciting hours every day during summer, always obediently runs to the door upon hearing his name called, however, he says: "If it's light and warm I'm happy staying out here, thank you!" then off he joyfully skips.

As the long, hot days grow cooler, Woody creates a cosy nest amongst dry montbretia leaves for basking in late autumn sun. But when winter chills arrive, perhaps horrible memories flood back and haunt him, reminding him of life as a homeless stray.

Then, trips outside are both perfunctory and brief, and when the east wind blows, pleading, wide-eyed at the window he urgently begs: "Please let me in! My ears hurt with the cold!"

One lazy day, when Woody was blissfully snoozing in a basket, a very rough, hostile-looking, battle-scarred tom cat's black head unexpectedly appeared, glaring menacingly

through the window. Fixing his mean, yellow, malevolent eyes on Woody (still the smallest cat at the hotel and one he may have thought perhaps he could replace), on discovering the door ajar, rapidly dashed inside uninvited, leapt onto his chosen victim, biting and overpowering him in a sudden, terrifying assault. Fur flew in the frenzied chaos, and as Woody, (still half-asleep), was knocked tumbling into the air, the assailant savagely kicked him and a jet of urine shot up in an arc. In seconds the humans' horrified voices were loudly screaming and shouting, flapping their arms, chasing away the opportunistic intruder, who thankfully never returned. "Oh, you poor little thing" she stroked him, checking the stunned but unharmed kitten, and went quickly to firmly  close the opened door and check the attacker had definitely gone. The woman laughed merrily when she returned: Woody luckily appeared to be none-the-worse for his ordeal and was rummaging excitedly through her wool bag. He seemed to have totally forgotten his so-recent trauma: "I think I will just play with your largest ball of wool for a while".

When Christmas-time arrived, Woody had been thoroughly trained by Brock, and the humans could see the energetic pair made a formidable football team. After playfully removing the shiny baubles from the tree together, they delighted in many frisky, fun sessions, but the sparkling, sequinned fairy luckily remained too high, even for them.

Spring returned, and with warmer weather Woody emerged from his hotel hibernation and enjoyed going out into the garden again. One beautiful, bright day, a lovely, striped cat was noticed early, sitting on a low wall with Brock. He was a friendly, familiar, older local cat, and, after a good breakfast Woody joined them both outside.

However, curiously, hours later he seemed to have completely disappeared: he didn't run with his happy skip to the door, as is his usual swift response when he hears his name being called. Sure he would return for his evening meal, his absence saw the humans becoming increasingly concerned, and they began to wonder, had someone taken him away?

The local children were asked (just in case he was with one of them), but they hadn't seen him either – no one had that day, so posters were hurriedly distributed and fixed on the gate: 'REWARD, MISSING'.

By eight o'clock in the evening the humans were worrying even more, there was no sign of Woody at all, anywhere, until suddenly, there he was! Casually sauntering down the path, returning to where he had been last seen first thing that morning, and he was still with the older, stripy cat too!

As Woody made his way to the hotel door, the other cat patiently watched, and, pausing to see the youngster go safely inside he set off, presumably back home to his own place. Strangely, the next day exactly the same thing happened – his new friend called early, then Woody, as if waiting, ran to enthusiastically accompany him, and disappeared again for hours and hours and hours, and all at once the humans realised: he was showing a young cat the ways of the world – Little Woody had grown up!

"PHEEEEW! What is that dreadful smell!" the humans were holding their noses, and the cats were reeling, distracted and shocked, the polluted room was positively reeking! Woody had sprayed on the sitting room curtain! It was the most pungent, stinky, fetid spray a cat could ever make! The hotel's little lovable and adored kitten was suddenly behaving like a real adult cat, a terrible, revolting, pongy tom cat! Even before the big clean-up began, the woman urgently dashed to the phone and made a call to the vet for an early appointment next day. Soon back, Woody, on returning home was just as popular with everyone again: peace had successfully been restored as well as the fragrant ambience at the hotel.

Inclined to be a little plump over the winter months, he gets called stocky and sturdy quite often: Woody can't bear chilly weather and suffers with cold ears, so on those days, wisely, he does love a warm basket! Luckily, he becomes more active with long summer days of excitement, and then tones up a little, although naughtily, he still asks for titbits of toast or cheese, sometimes. So, if you're ever along this way by the Cats' Hotel, and a charming (slightly rotund) cat with creamy, smoky-coloured fur greets you, whatever he says, please, promise you won't give him any treats!

Intrepid Elfie
The fearless explorer

The untidy skip stood outside the corner shop during its re-fit and each day it was steadily getting fuller, but as the small, bandy black kitten observed this point she thought miserably: "My stomach is getting emptier! Why has no one noticed me yet?" Christmas week was here and everyone was busy, rushing about preparing for the special day. Finally one passer-by stopped and stared, at last – someone had seen her! And, over the sounds of banging hammers and whirring saws from inside she could hear a woman's voice calling to one of the workmen: "Does this kitten belong here?" and he replied "Don't know where it came from, but I do know it's very noisy, and it's been here for several days".

Suddenly scooped up, the little cat was placed on a wall as the woman re-arranged her bulging shopping bags over one arm, and she was then placed securely in the other. "Who are you? And where are we going? Will you feed me?" enquired the kitten brazenly, and to make absolutely sure the woman knew exactly who the boss was, she nipped her hand

with rather sharp teeth. "Hey! What was that for?" the only reply was a bold, hard yellow stare. Soon they went into a house: "Mum! Look what I just found behind a skip!", and "Hello Sophie! Hello Angus! Look! We have a little visitor!"

With one glance at the plump, well-fed cats, the kitten rapidly jumped disapprovingly to the top of highest kitchen cupboard, hissing and spitting. "I expect she's very hungry Mum" the woman reasoned, and reaching up high, a plate of food was promptly, placatingly set before the disturbing, dominant presence. This swiftly disappeared, then the loud, raucous voice that followed seemed strangely to come from a much bigger cat. "Oooo, you don't like that noise do you Angus? She doesn't look very pleased at all does she Sophie?" said the woman's mother. "Come down off that cupboard you funny kitten!"

"I won't, and I don't think I like it here at all!" the kitten noisily replied, and as quickly as she'd had that thought she was taken away to another house: "This is the Cats' Hotel and here you'll fit in better: we'll go and see the vet tomorrow: you have a cold, and one of your eyes has closed", she heard.

But, as she looked around and began spotting other cats of many shapes and sizes, she wasn't sure at all, and set up her loud, persistent wailing song. One by one the cats left the room and the kitten didn't care in the least. The woman came and stroked her and was rudely rewarded by an ungrateful hiss and a little nip. "I will call you Elfie! I am sure the elves threw you out because you were too naughty even for them!" "MIIAAOOWEEURGH!" was the harsh, dismissive response. Patiently examining her, the vet was explaining "No, I'm sorry, but she will never have sight in that eye: she was actually born with it closed, and now (she is about five months old) it is too late". None of this care and attention was appreciated at all – totally uncooperative, Elfie angrily bit and scratched him. "I'll treat her cold and soon she should feel happier" he said.

But happy she wasn't: each day the Cats' Hotel seemed to get smaller yet Elfie didn't get much larger. It also became a lot less peaceful: "I really think I need to explore, these cats here are so dull and I know it must be much more interesting out there!" she mused, as she perched on a high spot near the back door gazing wistfully towards the garden. And spotting a big bunch of keys in the lock she began to relentlessly bash them with a very determined paw: "Open up! Let me out! I don't want to be in; I want to be OUT!"

Quiet days, quiet evenings and especially quiet nights became a memory with Elfie around. Long hours of leaping vertically to grab the humans' bedroom door handle, scratching frantically and wailing piteously became the new sounds of the night. And never seemingly tired, Elfie filled her days with frustrated, disgruntled complaints and constant key-bashing. "I don't like rules and I'm still not sure whether I like anyone here!" said the anti-social kitten, and no one could be sure either if they stroked her: would she scratch, bite or hiss, or maybe this time, just glare?

Largely ignored by the discomposed residents – difficult in itself owing to her constant squawking complaints – only excepting Woody, whose tolerance now reached new heights. Elfie wasn't bothered: any of the cats' company in her opinion was no substitute at all for that of people.

Better after her bad cold, and bursting with unbridled excitement, the day had come at last! Freedom! "Miaoowheeeeee!" The world outside beckoned with all the exciting people and new places, and off she enthusiastically toddled up the lane. The hotel grounds are fine for other cats, but certainly not for her, and it was readily discovered, Elfie's boredom threshold is very low indeed. Not far from the hotel runs a busy main road that cuts right through the village and most cats go in the opposite direction...............but not Elfie!

Upstairs, very soon afterwards, the woman was near an open window and heard irate female voices floating up on the breeze – "Get out of here! Shoo! Shoo! Shoo! Ooooo! It's only got one eye!" Dashing up the lane to investigate, she saw a furious hairdresser brandishing a broom, and an even more furious small cat defiantly standing at the entrance to the Ladies' Hair dressing Salon with four firmly planted feet, facing her boldly, and her huge, bushed-out tail was swishing crossly from side to side. "She's caused chaos! Just marched in here and has been rummaging through the clients' handbags. Is she yours?" Accusations hanging heavily in the air, the wriggling, very unwillingly restrained, complaining small captive was swiftly scooped up and returned back to the hotel.

The woman began to notice the unusually gregarious kitten dashing up to people in the lane, demanding in discordant tones that they stroke her and stop for a chat. Without doubt Elfie possesses a certain allure and an engaging, although rather quirky personality. She was sternly warned: "You are too friendly and too fearless when outside Elfie! You mustn't constantly approach strangers, seeking their attention".

Whenever the phone rang, Elfie began dashing to answer first, often knocking the receiver off and thoroughly confusing the caller with her irritated, loud protest when shooed away and placed on the floor, disappointed on discovering it wasn't for her. "I am important! Notice me! And – I don't like it either when you read the newspaper!" she angrily said, and regularly proved it with her pointed teeth as they sank like needles into the backside of the startled woman, quietly reading, who enquired: "Are you the most bad-tempered cat anywhere?" – and a fractious little face glowered defiantly back.

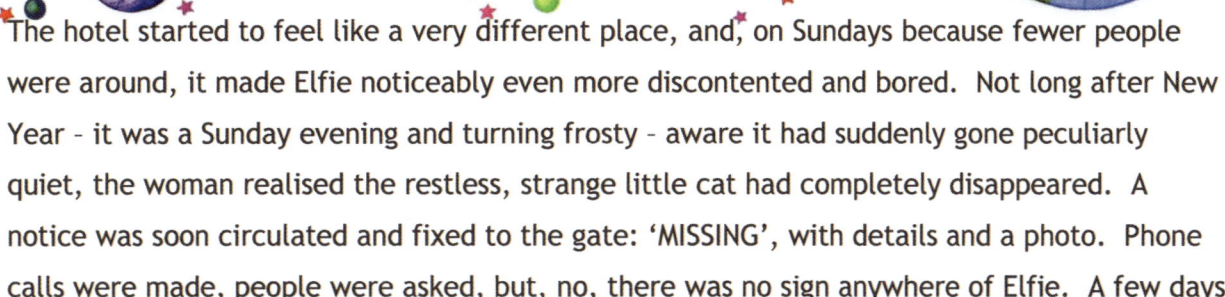

The hotel started to feel like a very different place, and, on Sundays because fewer people were around, it made Elfie noticeably even more discontented and bored. Not long after New Year – it was a Sunday evening and turning frosty – aware it had suddenly gone peculiarly quiet, the woman realised the restless, strange little cat had completely disappeared. A notice was soon circulated and fixed to the gate: 'MISSING', with details and a photo. Phone calls were made, people were asked, but, no, there was no sign anywhere of Elfie. A few days later she was still absent, until a call to a vet much farther away brought surprising news: they had seen her! A teenage boy called Wayne had found her crying pitifully outside a fish and chip shop several miles from home, hungry and lost. Loving animals, he gave her some of his fish, put her inside his coat and took her home. Wayne was almost as weird as Elfie: the humans were told later he was living in an old car in his grandmother's garage and had left his friends' address with the vet he had visited.

Calling there in the evening, a kind, helpful young couple answered the door with their Doberman dog at their side: it was a flat on the seventh floor. "Oh, yes, the little black cat, Wayne took her to the vet where they operated on her eye, but couldn't help". Hearing those awful words the humans' hearts sank as they dreaded to think what might be. "She has made good friends with our dog and loves sitting on the ledge gazing out of the open window of our high-rise!" they cheerfully related. Soon after, sending two of their other friends to the garage to fetch her, the small wanderer appeared again. In dismay, the humans immediately noted Elfie had a brand-new cold, her eye looked very worrying, and, seething with anger having being plucked from her big adventure, a very irascible, hotly protesting cat was returned to the hotel.

The new cold was severe and slow to go, and as a result of the ill-judged operation an eye-infection had set in. The long, hard battle to regain her health began and, needing eight further operations, Elfie was confined indoors, demented and desperate for long, long months. Forlornly gazing out of the window, only going out to see the vet, regularly (and always grumpy with him), Elfie sat vigorously bashing the bunch of keys hanging in the door: "Open up! Let me out! I don't want to be in, I want to be OUT!"

"What excitement is there here?" stridently complained Elfie. And, distracting herself, soon she demonstrated yet another curious quirk with unsheathed claws threateningly ready: "I can expertly stalk, tease and kill the elastic bands I manage to magically find, and I will scratch the hand that wants to take them from me, but I AM SO VERY FED UP!"

Eventually, she was well, and released, was trotting off rapidly: but this time she wore a lovely pink collar which had a barrel attached with her name, address and phone number – just in case! Within an hour the hotel received a call:

"It's Julie here from the big timber yard: do you have a small black cat with one eye? Yes, well she's been running around amongst the machinery and showing no fear. It's very dangerous! Please can you come straight away and collect her?"

Brought back once more to the tedium of the hotel, Elfie's squalling grievance was always the same: "I don't want to be inside! Let me out!" and in no time an angry, eager cat was swiftly scurrying off happily again.

The phone rang and this time it was the nearby garage: Suzie the secretary, concerned, explained: the small one-eyed cat was in her office and had been friskily darting between the large, moving vehicles in their yard. Urgently dashing to collect her, Suzie smiled and called "Come on Elfie", and from behind her desk out she obediently trotted, reserving all her bad temper for the woman who had so cruelly curtailed her fun.

Soon after the lure of the even busier main road with all its cars, buses, people and shops drew Elfie like a magnet: "MeeeeOOOW! What a lovely exciting place!" Warmly welcomed by Peter in the Pet Shop, the woman was told he had a cage just for her if she tired of lying in the window.

Popular with kind Ken the Green Grocer, she made lots of friends wherever she chose: "Everyone is so much more fun than in the hotel!" thought Elfie.

One day a knock brought the Pharmacist: standing solemnly on the front step in his white coat, he was carrying a large cardboard box out of which a small, cross black head was indignantly protruding. Only a few days later an old lady (showing considerable bravery), nervously knocked whilst struggling to contain and return an irate, snorting captive she'd found loitering in a nearby car park. Then, a day or so later, a young mum with her family in tow was dashing for a train, but, she informed the woman, Elfie had been waiting with the crowds standing at the pedestrian crossing by the side of the busy road, and the children had begged her to return the (now unfortunately infamous) kitten home to the hotel.

Worrying reports began to reach the hotel of the latest fun place for Elfie to casually observe the main road: perched precariously on the narrow top edge of the barrier railings!

As before, Sundays were always a concern – the Newsagent phoned: Elfie, now confined in the shop's back yard amongst empty lemonade bottles, had been taken there by two young girls who found her going into church. This was almost the final straw because determined Elfie had actually succeeded in crossing over the dangerous main road!

An early appointment at the vets the next day, with another cat, was only a short walk away which involved crossing over the steps of the big Railway Bridge. Shocked: the woman immediately saw a familiar small cat waiting there calmly on the station platform, mingling nonchalantly with the passengers and about to board the train for the city – Elfie! Quickly grabbed just as the train was running into the platform, and swiftly taken hotly protesting back to the hotel, she now knew: some solution was urgently needed with this wild, wayward spirit.

"I was going to have an adventure! – You have spoilt it!" Elfie's scowling face swore even more loudly than usual. "I wasn't afraid: it was fun! I am different! And by the way: when is that nice dog coming to visit again? I was the only cat here who didn't run away frightened!"

The long lead tied to a stake in the garden seemed worth a try, but, Elfie's keen eye saw spiders on the fence, and jumping just that little bit too far away, the next-door neighbour's panicked cries of alarm were heard right away and luckily in time to rescue the dangling adventurer, nearly strangled on the other side. Buying her a harness and lead, the humans set

off hopefully along the country lanes and nearby fields. "I love those horses and the sheep, but insist: I must look down every garden path on the way there!" The planned outings became impractical and exhausting, so she was taken next to wild meadows and a very long lead was used. Suddenly tiny Elfie disappeared: she became invisible amongst the flowers and tall grasses, and the humans couldn't see where she was!

It was then decided best to build a large, secure enclosure in the hotel garden with ladders, runs and perches, a deck chair for sunny spells and an umbrella too, where she can go anytime she likes. And luckily Sarah arrived to live nearby and came to visit her often, and she is a very lively little girl who adores cats. Elfie now has a lovely, laughing friend for company inside her special place, so she never gets bored.

They do say there is only one boss in the kitchen, and in the hotel she's small, black, stubborn and also very fierce when thwarted! Particularly fond of butter, she will leap to forbidden work surfaces (unlike the other well-behaved residents), and lick knives in order to relish any remaining traces. Her tiny nostrils crave steam inhalations, and although in her element at the woman's bath time, she regularly has to be chased away when found hugging the electric kettle. If another cat is careless when making use of the litter tray, it causes Elfie much undisguised irritation, and crossly, in a piqued and disapproving demonstration, she noisily tidies up.

Still assertive and given to baleful staring, she is slightly more reasonable these days: "Well, if another cat lies in my favourite bed, I won't bite (often), but of course I will stomp and trample and awkwardly lie on top of them!"

Now, with her firm friendship with clever Chester (a very home-loving cat), things have thankfully changed. They sleep together, tangle, tumble and tussle in play, and with her huge, wide, exceptionally bushy tail, Elfie adopts a threatening pose with her special pal, and, at times, mischievous accomplice.

The crazy miscreant extrovert contents herself these days with meeting new people inside the hotel, and has calmed her wild clawing and scratching to more socially acceptable and infrequent levels. But the only effective, offensive weapon the humans know to employ with this tyrannical cat when she is supremely obstinate, is to persistently blow and blow and blow on her!

This diminutive chum certainly has many moods, yet can sometimes now be a surprisingly loving cat.

Elfie even seems to miss the humans when they go out: she impatiently paces up and down on the ledge at the window telling every passer-by: "They've left me again!" and, ripping another hole in the net curtain, she will always be first to see them returning home.

The smallest cat with the biggest personality in the Cats' Hotel is gradually getting a bit better every day: the woman keeps thinking, it won't be long now, soon she will understand the word "NO!"

Clever Chester
The cat who can tell the time

Chester opened one eye, and looking quickly around, didn't like what he saw, so he closed it again. Perched on top of an untidy heap of discarded clothes, towels and newspapers he thought to himself: "At least I'm out of the way here", but he was wrong! Screams, higher and more piercing than usual were getting rapidly closer, and, without warning, the children of the house burst in and sprawled on top of him in noisy, arguing confusion. Almost suffocating, Chester was too fed up and too well-behaved to use his claws; somehow wriggling free he saw daylight, and unnoticed, swiftly made his way downstairs. "Maybe there's some breakfast for me" he hoped.

The kitchen was hot, the television was blaring on full volume, and the people were shouting loudly over sizzling bacon and sausages. Disturbed as usual by the scene, Chester nimbly trotted to his dish, "Oh no – it's empty again" he said, wrinkling his nose at the remains of last night's food (which arrived far too late) – and was still stuck around the edges. No one paid him the least bit of attention, "I'm not appreciated here" he said to himself, "I know I deserve something better."

Chester was still a kitten, a very good-looking one too, and was showing all the signs of super cat intelligence. Every day he was getting cleverer and cleverer, but in this house no one had noticed. "They don't even notice either" he thought, irritated, "that all the clocks are showing different times".

Going outside into the garden, Chester looked again at the neglected place and today he disliked it even more than usual, it was the most unloved garden in the whole road. "Old cars

and motorbikes and bits of metal won't grow! They'll never interest the moths and butterflies or the birds", and, of course, it was true, besides, they smelt horrible. There was just one fragrant patch at the bottom where a wild old lavender bush grew, and carefully making his way through the jungle of rubbish, Chester quietly dozed there for a few hours.

Then he had an exciting dream: there was a house, tidy, but not too tidy, with a nice garden full of flowers and bushes and benches and things, and cats were sitting, lying and washing here and there: and this was what Chester really liked – it was so quiet he could hear the birds singing, and the bees were buzzing about all over the flowers.

He woke suddenly – a bee was droning right by his ear – "Oh, it was a dream! Or was it?" he wondered. "I'll go back inside, I'm hungry, and see if there's any food, though it's so late now I couldn't possibly call it breakfast, I suppose it will be lunch". Dismay hit him hard: there on his unwashed plate lay a few pieces of gristly bacon and a chunk of burnt sausage, and even worse, flies were crawling happily over it. "Disgusting! They should know I do not like fatty food, especially on a dirty dish!"

Before he could dwell on his miserable thoughts, the young voices were shrieking again "Yipee! Easter Eggs!", and the boxes were flying around the kitchen. But then, without warning, the biggest boy (who never took much notice of Chester), ran in his direction and shoved an empty Easter Egg box right over his head, and roughly pulling his tail, laughed and laughed and laughed. No one said "Don't", or "That's naughty", or anything.

Swiftly escaping, Chester hurried outside, and, after a quick wash he then felt cool and composed. "Today I'm leaving here, I'm going to find my dream", said Clever Chester, "I know I will".

Following a long, straight road, he was excited: thirsty, hungry, but most of all excited. Chester hoped he'd find his dream soon. A few hours later he'd walked a long way, and then, beginning to feel rather tired, he paused and looked around wondering which road to go down next. Suddenly he felt unsettled, he could see two children and they were coming directly towards him: "Oh no, what will these two do to me?" he thought, perplexed. But as he was carefully picked up, Chester was amazed by how gently the girl stroked his fur, in just the right kind of way. "Aah! He looks lost: oh, isn't he lovely Nathan? I wish we could keep him!" she said to her younger brother, "So do I Michelle, but you know how unfriendly our Sophie is with other cats – perhaps we could find him a home?" Turning together into a lane off the main road, Chester was surprised by how the little girl held him: she didn't squeeze or grab him by the front legs; she wasn't rough at all. "I'm glad to give my paws a rest" he thought, relaxing, "they'll take a bit of washing later, but I can do that in my dream house!"

Soon the children were knocking on doors, enquiring: "No, sorry"; then at the next house "We've got dogs"; and further along the lane: "I work away from home". It was all sounding hopeless. Until being carried up the path of the next house, Chester found himself admiring the lovely spring flowers.

And all of a sudden he wasn't worried at all; he was serene and calm, and, being very clever anyway, quietly confident. As the door to this house opened a smiling woman exclaimed: "Ooo! What a beautiful kitten! I've always wanted a ginger one! Does he need a home?" The children explained. "Well thank you both very much! He is the best Easter gift I could ever possibly wish for!" she said. Chester's heart was beating faster, and, within a minute he was trotting purposefully along the hallway and into the first room. There were lots of other cats already here! Did they know he was coming? Maybe! None of them moved, they just silently said 'hello' by way of acknowledgement in the friendliest and quietest way, and Chester knew immediately – this was his perfect, dream home and where he was meant to be. Glancing briefly, he saw it was really quite tidy, with proper beds and baskets for cats, and, spotting a large, unoccupied plump velvet cushion, Chester happily settled down; "I'll have a quick nap now and eat later; I'm sure they'll serve good food here that I'll like".

And they did: lots of different, extremely tasty things put out three times a day, and always on clean dishes. "Welcome to the Cats' Hotel Chester!" the woman warmly said.

"This is all very well, it would be absolutely perfect, but there is just one thing; I owe it to all my friends in my new dream house!" decided Chester firmly. His special talents were developing fast. Aware that cats like routines, Chester looked at the big clock, and he had noted: on Monday breakfast was at 7 o'clock, Tuesday served at 7.10, Wednesday late, at 7.30, Thursday at 7.05 and Friday very late – 7.45! As for Saturday and Sunday, well – these 8.30s and 9 o'clocks disturbed him. It wasn't too bad usually at lunch time: the human had her sandwich at midday, but the evening meal! It was arriving anywhere between 4.30 and 6.30! No, it wouldn't do, the casual service must change, and clever pernickety Chester knew he was just the cat to sort it out.

The residents were uniformly compliant, understanding his particular, unique qualities. Charming Chiki was easy: she adores his fine good looks and smart, marmalade fur. Little Elfie, black and with one eye, admires his keen intelligence, and Woody, the big grey and white one, loves all the cats and is always ready to tuck in to another meal, anytime, and the sooner the better too. For Filthy Wify, anything to do with more food is of great interest: he was starving when he arrived at the hotel, and is only slowly adjusting. So with his authority fully accepted the whole gang gathered, and having listened carefully to Clever Chester, they were easily persuaded and ready to follow his plan.

With his glinting green eyes keenly following the hands on the big clock, at the stroke of seven Chester's new regime commenced. Elfie began leaping wildly at the door handle and noisily banging on the bedroom door. Chester's sharp claws were expertly shredding and lifting the carpet, and, using his surprisingly loud voice, he showed Woody and Wilfy and the others just how to be extremely vocally annoying to snoozing humans. "Soon they will be up and about and will feed us!" he had predicted, and he was absolutely right, they were, almost right away!

The following Saturday morning they were all assembled ready to demonstrate outside the humans' closed bedroom door, "Right! Now! It's 7am and that is breakfast time!" said Chester with uncanny accuracy. The loudest, least tuneful voice belonged to Little Elfie, and Squeaky Chiki was easily able to hit a suitably high, piercing note. Filthy Wilfy followed Elfie's example and enthusiastically threw his big, bulky body against the door –

bang!
bang!
bang!

And – just to make sure they were making their point, Chester vigorously scratched the carpet too! It worked perfectly, and he was extremely pleased with himself.

Tomorrow's Sunday, thought Chester critically, "and humans and Sundays are very unpredictable!" And despite her attempts at bribery with weekend midnight treats, the woman failed completely: the cats saw this tasty bonus as an extra perk negotiated by their undisputed new hero.

A month or so later, every cat was fully trained to Clever Chester's complete satisfaction: all he had to do was watch the clock, tick tock, tick tock, give his command: "7 o'clock: now!" Or when the humans were busy in their private work rooms and so engrossed they were unaware of time passing and the little grumbling cats' stomachs – "5pm, dinnertime – now!"

Very proud of himself, he doesn't expect much in return; if another cat catches a mouse, well of course it's Chester's mouse!

Preferring an indoor tussle with the snake draught excluder, they all know, if he really wanted to, he could easily catch something.

This cat champion displays a very pronounced love of home, driven equally by his loathing of having wet feet outdoors, and his endless curiosity: Chester

is certain that if he is away for long, he might miss something that would be to his distinct advantage.

If the humans leave any fish in the kitchen, unguarded, when there's a knock at the door, or their phone rings – it's understood, "It's all for me, especially if it's prawns: what's yours is mine" says Chester, "and what's mine is my own!"

Eyeing up the (by now) rather large, tatty hole in the carpet outside the humans' bedroom door, the woman and Chester agree: "Well, it was quite tidy there once" she says, "but it's only carpet, some cats just can't help being clever!"

After all, when the big fat bluebottles frantically buzz around the house in summer, who's the fastest fly catcher here? The woman watches in admiration as, with super  speed and agility, he vigorously chases in energetic pursuit of such delicious morsels. Buzz, munch, crunch, gone! "Thank you Chester!"

"I don't know if it's having only one eye: I've tried training Elfie at fly catching but she just seems to rip holes in the net curtains, so I have to do it all myself" he heroically says.

And, although always aloof with the woman if other residents are watching, his air of cool detachment completely dissolves when they are alone, and gleefully purring appreciatively as she rubs his little pink nose, she knows and he knows: in fact, it's generally agreed, he's a very Clever Chester.

Filthy Wilfy
The cat who can't keep clean

Wondering whether he'd ever find any food today, young Wilfy wearily said, "I've been through every single cat flap round here, and there's nothing left for me!" Sadly, and feeling very hungry, Wilfy found a quiet, sunny spot where he lay down and watched the birds. "If only I could catch one I wouldn't feel so empty".

He saw all the fat pets from the houses returning home still full after their breakfasts: they'd lazily ambled around their gardens and some only just managed to squeeze through their cat flaps.

"They are all bigger than me" thought Wilfy woefully, and although he didn't say so himself, they were all very much cleaner too. Wilfy washed his whiskers and face; now, if you just saw his head, you wouldn't say "What a grubby cat!" But being separated from his mother too soon, the only washing lesson he'd had was whiskers, ears and mouth.

He stretched out trying to snooze, his long legs and grimy paws felt tired, his dull coat didn't shine in the sun, and you could see his ribs quite clearly.

A mouse ran past his ear through the long grass, "Oh, I'm sure that would do nicely for breakfast – if only I could catch it" he said, but he'd also missed all the 'how to catch' lessons, so there was no chance of that.

Today though, something was different, it was Wilfy's first birthday and he'd had an idea: "All these cats around here are a bit too greedy, I'll travel and see if my luck changes!"

So, hungry but excited, Wilfy started his journey, keeping close to hedges and hiding behind fences: because he knew what would happen if he met humans, especially the little ones. They'd point and say "Ooooh! What a dirty cat! Did you ever see such a thin, scruffy thing?", or "That's the filthiest, skinniest stray in town! It must be! Our Tiddles would make two of him", and so on, and Wilfy didn't want anything to spoil today: already it felt special.

Now he had wandered so far, he was in a new, strange place, and ravenous Wilfy could hear his stomach rumbling and his feet were getting very sore, but still he carried on. Suddenly he stopped, amazed, and looking in astonishment at the house, he could see cats in every window and in the garden as well!

"I can't hear any hissing, growling or spitting, and I'm sure I can smell food too!"

Cautious but excitedly, he bravely strode straight through the gate, and up the path passing several cats, one or two of whom Wilfy noticed looked reassuringly just a slight bit tatty. He then saw there were cupboards outside like little houses, and they had nice dry beds inside. And, then he saw a brick outhouse furnished with carpets and cushions, and here and there were toys and catnip mice. It all looked very exciting and different to anything he'd ever seen before.

"All I need now is some of that delicious food I can smell" Wilfy thought optimistically, then, almost in the blink of an eye, a whole plateful was set beside him. Although surrounded by many cats, none of them tried to pinch it, and, with an audience of watchful eyes, he gobbled it all up. "Yum, this will be perfect if I can have a nice snooze now and wake up and find I'm not dreaming."

Exploring further and finding an inviting, empty striped canvas deckchair, Wilfy jumped up. For the first time in many weeks his stomach no longer growlingly complained, and as he lounged he drifted swiftly off into a sweet, settled sleep. Waking up a while later he heard soft, kind human words: "Don't be frightened skinny little stray! There's room here at the Cats' Hotel for you", and a comb was gently removing all the horrible, nasty things – encrusted dirt and lumps of congealed oil – from his coat. "I have found a home at last!" Wilfy contentedly whispered.

Quickly he made a lovely new friend, so Wilfy became yet another resident to fall under Woody's gentle, calming spell, and they were instantly the very best of pals. Wilfy carefully watched him and learnt how to thoroughly wash all the other bits, and before too long his coat was glossy and clean. After some weeks the woman admiringly said "You were grey and brown when you came! Now you're black and white and becoming very handsome!" And, devouring three tasty meals each day his body was growing bigger and bigger.

"I'm so happy, I'll be brave today and go inside the house and explore" Wilfy brightly decided. But his mood of curiosity changed rapidly as he discovered it was confusing and a very different, odd sort of place, compared to the gardens and rough land he was used to. Ever inquisitive, Wilfy rushed around cheerfully for a short while, boldly exploring, then agitated and suddenly panic-stricken, would present himself, urgently begging release from the unaccustomed confinement.

For some time this pattern was repeated many times each day! Off he would hurriedly dash out of the back door only to reappear crying at the front door a few minutes later: "Can I come in please?" However, his purposeful intent vanished when the door was closed, and Wilfy, puzzled, ran to it, afraid: "Please! Please! Let me out!" and the human always did! Then he would re-enter once more, look excitedly around, greet the other cats, and after just a brief visit be heard, panicky at the back door, crying fearfully, desperate to escape. Soon feeling freshly confident Wilfy tried again, but after a few minutes distracted by the strangeness, he began feeling trapped. "Please let me out!" The woman laughed and said "We won't call you Wilfy any more, we'll call you Wilfy Yo-Yo!", and she opened the door. Eventually the day thankfully came when it wasn't quite so bewildering for him anymore. Wilfy can now settle for several hours, but is still really only happy to be in the hotel if he knows his human friends are also there.

Tearing tissues and newspapers to shreds to create a warm bed showed a rather feral trait which was swiftly rendered obsolete once Wilfy realised the instant luxury of chairs, cushions and baskets. Obviously he was completely unused to curtains: they appeared to present one of the more baffling aspects of his new life indoors. When they were drawn closed in the evening Wilfy had lots of fun hiding behind them. From this refuge he would emit loud chirrups trying to entice other cats to join him. Then, without warning Wilfy would suddenly hurtle out, leaping indiscriminately forth, his big feet clumsily crashing and colliding into cups, glasses and ornaments, leaving a trail of chaos and upturned tables. Thankfully though, in time Wilfy became more used to the weird novelty of his new environment and became much less ungainly when navigating the hotel's interior.

Just when Wilfy began to look perfect with a marvellous glossy coat, splendidly robust figure and perky eyebrows meeting in the middle, he enthusiastically scampered off as usual down the path at dusk. But this time Wilfy ventured to explore somewhere new – and then something terrible happened. Leaping over a fence at a garage, he slipped and felt himself helplessly falling straight into a big open-topped metal drum of thick, sticky brown oil. Scrambling desperately out, Wilfy dashed, terrified, back home, and as he reached the door, crying loudly "Help!" it opened, and immediately Wilfy ran in. The almost unrecognisable, grimy cat bore little resemblance to the glorious cat that had so recently gone out. Frantically he began racing about wildly, slithering all over the hotel from room to room, and every carpet and chair and cushion was quickly covered in sticky smudges and paw prints. "Help me!" said Wilfy, "I don't want to be this filthy!"

Horrified, and using up a whole kitchen roll, the woman wiped and wiped, but Wilfy was so dirty this time it didn't make any difference. Wilfy heard her concerned voice phoning the vet: "Yes, we'll try washing up liquid in the bath and bring him to the surgery first thing tomorrow". Wilfy was whisked up to the bathroom: he felt sick with shock and was shaking. Soon the bath had turned a different murky colour as a fiercely wriggling cat remained completely oil-soaked. And, over an hour later even after their constant, struggling efforts, with aching backs and arms the humans could see, it was utterly hopeless, he was still the muckiest cat in town, probably in the whole world. Wrapping up a hot water bottle in a towel, frightened, shivering, sad wet Wilfy was placed in a cat basket to spend his very first night indoors.

Later on the following day, the woman called back at the surgery to collect him, and she gasped at the truly remarkable transformation: Wilfy was gleaming, wonderfully restored to his former glory, and, luckily, he seemed none the worse for his ordeal. The vet told her his team had worked hard: it had taken two thorough shampoos, the oil was so deeply ingrained. Delighted, she exclaimed: "Oh! Wilfy! You look so handsome; your fur's dazzlingly white again!" The vet spoke firmly to the radiantly clean cat: "No more of this wandering at night! You must stay in and keep out of mischief!"

From that moment he was called Filthy Wilfy, which, as he is still rather an adventurous cat who is never deterred by wild, wet or windy weather, and often comes home distinctly grubby, has firmly stuck! After eating, he will spend an hour or more sprucing himself up, then it's time to go out and do it all again!

Unfortunately though, not long after this escapade Filthy Wilfy lived up to his name again! Doing a garden re-design project at the hotel the humans were prepared and ready, waiting one day for the arranged delivery of three cubic metres of ready-mix concrete which, due to the awkwardness of the location was to be pumped in from a big lorry in the lane. Once delivered, their plan was to lay pretty pebbles and gravel all over the surface using a large collection of many beautiful, old stones. As it arrived, they donned thick gloves and set to work raking the concrete level, and wading welly-deep with some difficulty through the heavy mass, they were busily absorbed arranging stones.

The humans worked in what seemed like a giant-sized, deep, wet cowpat, and from all of the hotel's windows, many cats were observing the changes with very curious eyes. Naturally, because the humans were outside, Wilfy was not indoors amongst them. Engrossed in the task, suddenly, helplessly, the woman caught sight of Wilfy running cheerfully and swiftly in inquisitive greeting towards her. With an athletic leap he launched himself on to the finished area, which at that stage was about six by twelve feet wide and had been surfaced by stones. Although it looked deceptively solid, it was actually still wet, and as Wilfy landed the pebbles began to sink and shift moving under his weighty bulk. A terrible look of panic quickly registered on his face, and as fast as he tried to run, Wilfy was slowing and sinking with each laborious and treacherous step. "Help!" Filthy Wilfy cried miserably, and struggling in terror, he reached the perimeter, but his four white legs and belly were covered thickly in grey concrete, and his usually swift paws were now clad in heavy concrete boots.

Quickly grabbed and hauled to the water butt, the woman instantly carried out urgent remedial washing, despite traumatised Wilfy's wriggling resistance. And five and a half hours later when the garden job was at last finished, a very subdued and stiffened cat was then forced to undergo the next stage of his thorough clean up. Filthy Wilfy hated the nail brush, and has a deep-seated fear of water and soap after his oil escapade, but there was no other way! Eventually after a long, difficult, wet, squirming struggle he was dried, and a fine comb was then used to remove the remaining concrete dust. So happily, Wilfy was restored to something more like his former condition, shaken but plainly relieved. As he scurried off a little later he paused, eyeing the location of the accident with deep suspicion, and leaving a very wide berth, quickening his pace, he swiftly ran past.

Back at home Wilfy looked around: there were lots of baskets and beds to choose from, "I'll have this one that's already nice and warm" he thought, and athletically jumping on top of

the sleeping occupant, it was easily done! Wilfy's grown so large and muscular the other cats don't dare to argue. "You're just like a massive kitten Wilfy! I'm afraid you don't know how heavy you are!" the woman knowingly says.

It took time for some of the other cats to get used to Wilfy's rather brusque ways. Rough and brawny, he will briskly run, fizzing with energy: leap with a flying tackle on top of another cat, give a firm-gripped, enforced three-second-wash, then wrestle wildly for a while, completely overwhelming the stunned, less robust and more refined residents. None of these actions were ever meant to be vicious, and the unfortunate recipients of this unsociable behaviour seemed aware of this fact and showed Wilfy they can be amazingly tolerant.

Wilfy has been called a hooligan, but the woman knew

his uncouth behaviour was really just kittenish fun, as if he is merely catching up on all that had perhaps been missing from his harsh early life.

It is rumoured Wilfy still nips through other cat's cat flaps. He does have a fear of some men (especially those that empty the bins), scurrying off panic-stricken to hide until they have gone. But he visits two special neighbours in their houses nearby, and both are charmed by his direct and friendly approach, so they always have a ready supply of food and biscuits, which alarmingly he never refuses. Gobbling up all the tasty titbits they save for him he always finishes every last little speck. At home (hunger still a haunting memory), the woman laughs: "Please slow down Wilfy", but he knows: if he wins the race, his dextrous paw can impudently slide another cat's dish his way! After every meal Wilfy spends lots of time vigorously polishing plates, retrieving tiny morsels missed by others, always completely absorbed, he is ever-hopeful.

With his lively tongue fishing about in empty food trays or tins, he triumphantly says: "I know I've got a gravy moustache, but I will be able to enjoy that later!"

A lady knocked at the door one day, and pointing at Wilfy she said "When are the new cat's kittens due?" He pretended not to have heard her.

Wilfy's become as big and round as those cats he used to enviously watch. His desire to sample whatever the woman is eating is hungrily expressed by loud purring, and his habit of drooling, whilst hanging his head an impolite inch from her plate anticipating the delight. At intervals his beautiful, steady green eyes beseech – and of course he certainly knows – sometimes she will oblige!

Rather impulsive, with boundless energy and a venturesome nature, his boisterousness with other cats at the hotel are really joyful displays of his excessive stamina. And always good-natured, Wilfy soon submissively washes the stunned cat he took by surprise in his over-enthusiastic excitement.

As affectionate Wilfy eagerly greets the woman, tunefully chirruping with tail erect, or lies on his back with his legs in the air, frolicking happily with a catnip mouse, in every way he is like a huge, adorable, irresistibly exuberant kitten.

Squeaky Chiki
The solitary singer

Today Chiki sang a quiet lament to herself: her lovely lady Valerie who she'd spent her whole life with so far had gone, and now things were being taken out of their house. Alan spoke to his wife "What will we do with Chiki? Mum loved her so much, but I'm sure our big dogs would eat her for breakfast". Luckily Alan was a postman and knew all of the houses on his round some distance away. Suddenly he had a great idea: "There is a place I know! It's a few miles from here and the people around there call it the Cats' Hotel. I'm not sure how many cats they already have, though: I wonder if I ask whether they might want another?"

Chiki sadly remembered kind, tidy Valerie, "Those cosy, happy evenings spent together in our warm home have gone and now I'm frightened, and I'm alone". It was a troubled, anxious evening, and that night Chiki tried to sleep on Valerie's empty chair for reassurance, but the night was long and lonely. Feeling further disturbed as morning came, she saw the furniture was now disappearing very quickly, including Valerie's chair, and the next thing that left the house was a cat basket, and Chiki was sitting nervously inside. "I said you were a good cat" Alan said reassuringly, "it will be alright, I have spoken to the woman and you are going to the Cats' Hotel now", and with that he closed and locked the door of her empty house behind them.

Arriving at the new place Alan had called 'The Cats' Hotel', Chiki saw a smiling woman standing in the doorway, and more cats than she had ever seen at once in her whole life, all curiously, silently staring at her with wide eyes: some looked from behind windows and others were in the hallway. "Welcome Chiki! I'll see if I can find you a good home. If you've never mixed with other cats, it might be rather difficult for you to fit in here" said the woman, who thanked Alan, then swiftly whisked Chiki up the stairs and into a big, quiet room alone.

Chiki agreed it was very pleasant: she saw a soft bed, toys, and a big window looking onto a lovely garden, and she patiently listened to all the instructions, her head tilted attentively. "I didn't use a litter tray at home, though" she thought, recalling how her old lady Valerie had laughingly applauded each time she popped into the sink for a wee: "Bravo! You are such a good, clever girl Chiki, saving me money!" Chiki liked her new bed, purred approvingly at the varied, delicious menu, and was enjoying her long chats with the new woman who said how pretty she looked. And to show her appreciation, Chiki gently grabbed the hand that was stroking with both paws and affectionately washed each finger in turn with her rough, pink tongue. Then, feeling more relaxed, Chiki rolled over on the table, and as the woman stroked Chiki's stomach, hearing

her squeak in delight, she exclaimed "You sound just like a dolphin! I'll call you Squeaky Chiki!"

Chiki's sweet disposition and quaint, mysterious gaze was so friendly – and soon settled, she began to show her demonstrative personality. It was immediately apparent she was used to, and loved, lots of attention, reciprocating with nose rubs and gentle head butts, accompanied by contented, cheerful chattering. She was suddenly starting to feel a lot happier again, although Chiki was aware that beyond the door to her new room many other cats also lived in the Cats' Hotel: "Are they friendly?" she wondered anxiously. "I have never made friends with another cat, but have been frightened and chased by a few".

The woman took her along to see the vet for a check-up and he noticed she had two broken front teeth which needed removing. But apart from that she was in good general condition and all Chiki required was regular combing.

Sometimes the other residents were often inquisitively posted outside her door attentively listening, and after a few days of polite, introductory chit-chat, Chiki decided the time might be right to sing them one of her special songs. Valerie was musical and always singing and humming tunes, and together with Chiki had spent many happy evenings listening to opera. "Perhaps my invisible audience will like it too!" And they certainly did! Woody, instantly impressed, replied straight away with a lovely variation on the aria, and Elfie joined in enthusiastically too (although loud, she was not quite so musically talented, Chiki observed). "Well, no one growled out there, so perhaps they won't be too unfriendly" Chiki thought, and she began to feel bright and hopeful.

"We don't need to find you a new home now Squeaky Chiki! You've been in here a week, and I think you have already found one!" And with those words the woman opened the new cat's private door leading into the hotel. Composed but now silent, Chiki calmly found her way downstairs, and going into the first room spotted an unoccupied cushion, quietly made her way to it, sat down and agreed "Yes, I like it here: I think maybe I really do belong!"

Almost immediately a very handsome ginger cat looked her way, came quickly across, washed Chiki's head once or twice, and suddenly Chiki thought, amazed: "I have a friend – I'm no longer a solitary cat!" And swiftly, a fantastically close friendship blossomed between them: her sweet, placid nature and good looks had clearly completely enchanted clever Chester!

With her four neat white socks, pretty face with black eyebrows and white whiskers, and gentle disposition, she readily charmed all the cats who seemed to agree: Chiki was very appealing, and soon she had made even more friends.

The evenings were very different for her now: once darkness fell, this little night owl habitually sprang to life! At ten o'clock every evening Chiki dashed to the door ready to go out. Usually, at 10 pm Valerie had gone to bed: "Goodnight bellissimo", and for five years each night, Chiki had enjoyed moon-bathing and midnight rambles, always prowling alone under the stars.

Daytimes were her snoozing time, and if she was ever outside in daylight, she always felt rather peculiar and nervous.

Now she heard: "You stay out as long as you want but make sure you return to the hotel before dark!" Still lured by the familiar scents of the night it was difficult to adjust, but slowly, quiet, secure secret places were discovered for sunshine dreaming. And luckily, if her nerve failed her in the garden at the Cats' Hotel, there was usually an open window to squeeze through, back to safety, and reassuringly, Chester, her brilliant best friend was there, because he never wanders too far away.

Obviously, she had grown up well-used to enjoying fun games on the stairs, and like a playful kitten, Chiki will not allow the woman to pass, monopolising her every time with gentle paws darting through the banister railings, as she firmly grabs her hand.

Passively she watches wildlife, whilst sitting inside on the window ledge, and, absorbing the morning sun, quietly sunbathing, Chiki dreamily observes the view.

Although Chiki has so quickly and obligingly learned to use the litter tray, soon she was spotted squatting in the wash basin having a long wee: "Now I know how you got your name!" the woman said, amused: "Use the nice clean tray!" and as she politely obliged afterwards: "I think I'll call you 'Piss-a-Pint' Chiki!"

Waiting, regularly looking as though she wanted to sit on the woman's knee, and sitting closely next to her, whilst meeting her eyes questioningly, Chiki kept being asked by her in a friendly way: "Why won't you hop up, Chiki?" And frequently puzzled at this apparent hesitancy, the woman often repeated the same enquiry. Chiki tilted her perky head and chattered her reluctance in explanation, but despite longingly gazing with her beautiful green eyes at the empty knee, still refused.

Then Alan, the postman, delivered a parcel one day and he explained the mystery: "My Mum Valerie was a most particular lady: a tidy hair-do, she always wore smart clothes, and she had a special cloth which she always placed across her knee to keep her clothes nice; "Now I am ready little darling! Come on, Chiki, you can sit on my knee!" she used to say". The new woman smiled understandingly and later on said: "Look Chiki! My clothes were very nice too (once). I know they might now have threads pulled and are often covered in cat hairs – but I don't worry, and I don't want you to, either. You are very welcome on my knee anytime!"

And so one day not so long after, Chiki, purring loudly, did just that, she finally understood: "Well, I did see a little difference; but I was just making perfectly sure and being polite!"

Chiki was enjoying life again; lots of favourite trout and tuna titbits came her way, always a much-appreciated delight for this little fish fanatic. And, as long as no one ever stands behind her when she is eating, slowly, daintily she enjoys it all. Usually, she is the last cat to finish a meal and the first to loudly purr with pleasure when meeting the woman's glance. And, if her opinion is asked on anything, tirelessly she graciously debates and discusses. Using her subtle sophistication and undisputed charm, Chiki has adapted so capably to her new life here at the hotel, and Chiki knew now for sure, she had found a lovely new home, and best of all, she wasn't alone anymore.

Queen Talitha
The regal cat of humble birth

Never fully asleep, the young cat kept as still as she could, trying to ignore the noise of cars, lorries and honking horns; and happy to have found the small car park, with its few shrubs at the edge, where she could rest in safety: wisely, it was only ever after dark she emerged.

In no doubt, it was definitely better than the steel works: everywhere in this city was noisy, and there were few places for a young cat to hide. "At least this spot is not as rowdy" she thought as the quiet office workers went one by one into their building, and most only returned to their cars later "and no one knows I'm here".

"I am thirstier and hungrier this morning. It will be a long wait until I can see if anyone has thrown anything by the bins tonight" she thought. Just then something caught her eye and she peeped through the thick shrubbery: a young man was standing, not far away talking rapidly on his phone whilst juggling a sandwich and a coffee. His voice was getting louder, and suddenly, looking cross, his hand went up and at that moment his sandwich flew to the ground. Stamping his heel, he was now sounding angry, and then turning his back, he rapidly disappeared.

The glistening, fat ham sandwich temptingly lay only a few feet away, and the hungry young cat could smell it: quivering with the thought of an unexpected early meal she hovered, hesitating (just briefly), and beginning to drool, she heard the piercing cry of a nearing sharp-eyed seagull. In an instant she pounced, and excitedly retrieving the welcome treasure, took it swiftly back to the safety of her dark hidey-hole in the corner to slowly relish.

It was always lonely, and with shorter days becoming cold now, often she felt hungry, especially on Mondays and Tuesdays when the city was quieter and fewer people were around in the evenings. The nearby restaurants and takeaway cooking aromas always teased her young nostrils: chicken, ham, and other delightful things too delicious to imagine floated alluringly on the air. Trying to make her bed in the dead leaves and wind-blown rubbish that had accumulated in her den, it had been another hungry night, and now she couldn't snooze or get warm. Then the rain came in heavy, prolonged, noisy showers: "My coat will be extra difficult to clean today" the young cat was sure.

A massive sneeze overtook her, then another and another; she hadn't even been aware of the lovely car arriving nearby, and the elegantly dressed accountant standing looking at her, concerned; "I don't feel so good" the weary cat decided. "Yes" the smart lady was saying, having quickly looked up the number of the nearest animal charity: "She only looks quite young to me, definitely a stray, and not well, behind the bushes in the corner of our small car park. Can you come soon?"

John arrived swiftly, and to him, caring and clever and quick, it was like any other day – he was always trying to do his best for the needy, homeless and distressed animals in this big city. Ill, the young cat was feeling unusually tired, she didn't resist his approach and was soon stowed away inside the white van. As it stopped some miles away outside the bustle of the city, John's phone rang: "An emergency? Yes, I will be there as fast as I can" and scooping the cat basket from the back of his van the kitten found herself, alone in the dark inside a big garage. Only dimly aware later she must have been asleep, she saw the glint of sunlight on John's glasses and his kind, twinkly eyes were smiling at her: "I didn't realise how lovely you were this morning! You are special, aren't you?" Standing a moment, John looked into her beautiful, gazing earnest eyes, saw the thick, dark fur and knew; "Sarah!" he called, and a smaller person with another bright beaming smile came her way, which made the young cat feel much better. "What do you think Sarah? Shall we keep this one? She is so gorgeous, isn't she?" With a squeal of excitement Sarah jumped up and down, delighted, and threw her arms around him: "Daddy! This is the best present ever! What name shall we call her?"

Talitha calmly snuggled up in the conservatory, and liked everything: the warmth, the quiet, the good regular food, and with love and care from John was soon well again and looking splendid. "I see you are going to have kittens young Talitha!" John observed and Sarah squealed again, even more thrilled at the thought of further furry feet arriving, and, taking a brush she gently combed Talitha's shining fur, singing a song. "When the kittens are born Sarah, you can choose their names!" There were four, all black and white and healthy: two girls and two boys. A lady who helped the animal welfare organisation that employed John had heard all about them; her house was miles beyond the city in a village; she had a grand place in the country: "Can I have the two boys when they are ready John, please, if that is alright with you?" And so it was arranged. The kittens, born in summer, contentedly enjoyed life inside the warm conservatory and as they grew, going out through the open door with mother exploring in the garden. Called Lucy and Maria, Sarah played with the young females for endless, energetic and happy hours, and Talitha, ever-watchful, was very proud and an excellent young mother.

"It's just us and the three girls" John told his daughter, and "I have some other news for you too!" Sarah, instantly curious, carefully listened. John was not only wonderful with animals, but incredibly skilled with plants too and had very green fingers. "We are leaving here soon and moving. I am going to run a Garden Centre Nursery where we will live, and it is in a place many miles away". "Will the cats come?" Sarah immediately wanted to know, "Yes, and they can catch the mice there!" John cheerfully replied, and so their new life shortly began.

Being surrounded by flowers and the smiling, chatting visiting gardeners was the opposite of Talitha's lonely young life in the bustling, dirty city, and instantly, it suited them all. The furry female trio loved their marvellous, interesting and colourful home: it was a thrilling new territory. Soon the sisters were both skilled at mousing and had endless fun playing hide and seek in sheds and poly tunnels. And at last proud Talitha was able to sit quietly in safe, tranquil surroundings, and with her glorious good looks, always groomed to perfection, she was appreciated and often much admired.

The Garden Centre backs onto the Cats' Hotel, and, with inquisitive eyes on both sides of the fence, introductions didn't take long, and feline friendships soon formed. Visits became regular: the Nursery cats eagerly explored and the young lively sisters Lucy and Maria shared their exploits with the hotel cats: butterfly chasing, bird watching and exciting greenhouse games. Talitha, more aloof, and serenely above the youngsters' play, watches imperiously, always distant with non-related cats, but welcoming humans' admiration and praise.

Any cat impudent or foolish enough to trifle with Talitha knows without doubt when they have got too close! People, yes, a-plenty, but only her daughters are allowed the privilege of familiarity; any other venturesome upstart will instantly feel the full force of her fearsome right hook. This well-tried and trusted deterrent is deftly employed to protect her privacy, and an air of exalted exclusivity pervades Talitha.

Sarah was seven, sociable and full of fun, enthusiastically playing for long, laughing hours amongst the cats and John's beautiful flowers. Sarah, also exceptionally bright, and a young mine of horticultural knowledge, able to identify all of the plants by both their Latin and English names, soon knew all of the hotel cats' names too, and they were often entertained by their new friend, both at the Nursery and the hotel. Elfie was more delighted than any cat, as during weekends and the summer holiday, and at any other available opportunity, Sarah attentively provided her with welcome games and jolly company inside Elfie's special enclosure.

Curious, the cats from the Nursery were spotted frequently in the hotel grounds, following Sarah, and visiting their new friends, so before long they were a familiar, welcome threesome.

When John and Sarah had locked up and gone home, the three cats began to gather at the hotel back door, politely sniffing the kitchen aromas. A patient, if insistent, fluffy throng, at

teatime or supper they often wanted a helping too! Soon, Talitha had trained her daughters to sing in unison, an urgent but harmonious prelude delivered beseechingly at mealtimes.

"Miiaaoowwyummmmmmmmmm! Miiiaaoowwwyummm!" As if reinforcing their request, the beguiling trio all hold up a paw in their uniquely entrancing entreaty. Of course, a little extra could always be found for the peckish family at the door! Then with plates empty and shining, a satisfied, contented alliance licks vigorously with their busy pink tongues, until mouths are clean too. All three, very partial to a drop of cream or cat-milk, enjoy the menu which occasionally includes this extra delight. Although Talitha quickly made it plain: titbits of cheese are very agreeable indeed, "Mmyyum!", but not on her account fish in any shape or form – she will visibly wrinkle her pretty offended nose, recoiling in total disgust "mmyyyuckpoo!"

As the weather turns cool, it becomes evident Talitha apparently recalls the pleasure of being indoors, out of the chill. With a detached but determined, superior manner, she strolled in one cold day, purposefully choosing a vantage point on a sofa from which she could observe, and if the need arose, repel any impudent intruders who might dare to invade her chosen space. Fearless as ever and looking tiny next to Talitha (always so grand and powerful), Elfie's immediate, bold approach was not appreciated. With her swift right hook, Talitha continually maintains her chosen isolation from all of the hotel cats.

When the weather outside is freezing, occasionally Lucy and Maria can be persuaded to briefly come inside and also enjoy some warmth in their mother's protective presence. And what a presence it is! With her huge, long white whiskers and small white moustache, every hair of Talitha's splendid coat seems to have been fastidiously groomed into place. Her thick fur is so soft with such a luxuriant lustre, it endows Talitha with immense, majestic beauty and an air of reserved exclusivity.

Serious, fearless and irascible, only the foolhardy would choose to tangle with Talitha. Highly territorial and with extremely sharp claws, she is a formidable and powerful adversary.

Taking great exception to a visiting, giant black poodle one day at the Nursery, she leapt into brave and immediate action. Pouncing on the dog, and not in the least daunted by its size, she executed a sudden, memorable attack, sending the poor, yelping hound scurrying off in haste, with its shocked owner running behind, never to return. Such pronounced, protective behaviour illustrates the seriousness she attaches in responding tirelessly to her important, maternal role.

 After a few years of running the nursery, one day John told Sarah then the woman of their plans to move away, quite a distance from here. This time, talented John was changing to yet another new career: he would soon be selling boats! They would be going to a Marina and living on water, and so the two people who had brought the feline family were about to leave this area.

After discussion it was decided that the best solution would be if Talitha, Lucy and Maria stayed in their now-familiar surroundings at the Garden Centre and came to the hotel for breakfast, lunch and tea. This was agreed by all as a fairly straightforward plan, because the trio were regularly around, never wandering too far away.

So, in preparation, an old, strong, wooden two-storey cupboard on legs was found and brought here, and its top was water-proofed. Then cat-sized holes were cut in its door, entry for the trio into its deep shelves which were furnished with cardboard boxes, newspapers, pillows and blankets where they can stay dry and safely shelter and sleep. There is also a converted brick out building here at the hotel, with safe beds if they fancy, as well.

Quite often Talitha chooses to be indoors at night, but for little Lucy and Maria it's still much more of a rare event. Fond of quietly sunbathing, spending most days outside, except when it's very wet or cold, she keeps a keen eye on her daughters, and sits or lies with them for hours, happily huddled together.

Talitha is a striking cat, and with her serene, regal bearing gives no hint of her hard city struggle when so young. With great attention to her grooming she presents an exquisitely tidy and immaculate appearance. This awesome cat can really glower and, freezing out all unwanted intrusions, will in her own haughty way, enjoy her quiet seclusion. She still rebuffs advances from unrelated felines, but when it comes to evening time, Talitha is secure, totally relaxed, and purring happily on the woman's knee, demonstrating her delight that she is well-loved, and definitely admired and appreciated.

Moody Maria
The quirky cat with two personalities

Cool and aloof in the morning: "I want to be left alone; I have things on my mind", Maria looked pensive and sad as she purposefully hurried off to one of her solitary hiding places. Only a few hours may have passed, and there she is, this time heading deliberately towards the woman: "Hello! Lovely afternoon!" and confidently with bold, purring overtures, Maria then demands undivided attention and being endlessly stroked, talked to and appreciated.

So insistent are her requests, it is as if this curiously contradictory cat is compensating in her quirky, suddenly capricious way, for that timorous, shy cat she so recently was. The defensive, reserved demeanour becomes transformed into a purring, congenial, perfect pussy cat! All too aware that her whim or the wind might quickly change, her wishes are happily met, making the most of moments spent in this strangely compelling cat's company!

When Maria's joyfully receiving affection she drools in delirious delight, bearing little resemblance to the adamantly distant introvert who crossly scuttled off earlier to retreat with such haste.

In contrast to her sister Lucy's blithe spirit, Maria is a much more complex personality. Having the softest, short coat imaginable (which thankfully is easily managed), she has a round and lovely head. And a rather quaint characteristic of Maria's is her curly corkscrew tail which she twitches and rotates crossly when irked, or if interrupted in her self-imposed seclusion.

And if approached when unsociable, she can be irascible with other cats, and will angrily berate any boisterous males who dare to bully or challenge her! "You think I look soft?

You're confusing me with another cat!" Whack! Skittish she may be, but there's a petulant paw ever-ready to demonstrate: Maria's definitely no pushover! She has inherited her mother Talitha's trait (though clearly Maria is a left-hander), and a swift left-paw swipe is often very effectively employed. This cat knows exactly how to reinforce her intolerance and ensure privacy.

And trained by Talitha, she is a strong third voice in the ritual mealtime choir trio, but Maria peevishly disapproves if interrupted at these melodious moments. It's her realm of absolute dominance, just outside the hotel back door is where she is the self-appointed boss. An innocent Woody, dashing past for his pre-dinner grass salad, will receive a hefty clout as Maria's voice emphasises her dislike, with an angry, unmusical wail.

When Wilfy and Chester mischievously tease or chase the sisters for a bit of naughty boy team sport, the playful pair may, at times, succeed in rattling little Lucy, but never her stout-hearted sister! With claws well honed on sheds and trees, the troublesome males are soundly routed by Maria's indomitable mighty paw.

Fearless and formidable, she proved one night just how territorial and brave she actually is. It was a dark and very wet winter's night, when suddenly the humans heard a disturbance outside: there was shouting and piercing animal screams, so quickly they dashed to investigate. Shocked, they could dimly see, only just visible against the darkness, the menacing outline of an intruder, with two agitated dogs, both of whom were being fiercely confronted and bravely attacked by Maria! And although not a particularly large cat, she was valiantly in the midst of the pair of wildly yelping terriers, scratching and fighting like a tiger.

"Get your cat off my dogs!" the suspicious character was desperately yelling, urgently wanting to escape. This amazingly heroic cat had given the would-be-thief and his dogs something very different to what he had probably envisaged. Prising her off her prey was not an easy task, and with Maria still in full fight mode, muscular and strong, hissing and spitting, she was eventually hauled off and carried quickly indoors. Alarmed, the woman dashed with her upstairs to quiet and safety, but in her distressed, adrenaline-filled, terrified state, Maria bit the woman's thumb and fingers several times.

Calming and commending her incredible feat of outstanding daring and bravery, an anxious examination revealed a dog bite on her stomach. And although relieved it was not any worse, it seemed amazing Maria was unscathed apart from this one injury which, at the surgery next morning the vet confirmed was the only evidence of this terrifying incident, and he then successfully treated her wound.

In order to keep a watchful eye for a while and offer much due praise, the woman decided she deserved a confined week's holiday inside the hotel. And as if aware, and unusually, uncharacteristically compliant, Maria then calmly enjoyed endless hours of fuss and special treats. "I don't really like being inside, I prefer greenhouses with walls that I can see through. But – just for now: I am a tiny bit tired today and do have a few aches and pains. And thank you for giving me a room with a big window so I can keep an eye on the grounds for you!"

It was a good opportunity for her to have some well-earned rest and recuperation and recover from her ordeal, and soon Maria was luckily restored to her determined, quietly dominant self.

Having spent most of her young life enjoying the exciting activities of the Garden Centre with her mother and sister, most of the time Maria makes it quite plain: she still loves the open air.

When at evening the gardeners have disappeared, she likes lounging on shelves in sheds and snoozing in greenhouse nooks, or perhaps the cats' cupboard at the hotel: just so long as it is outdoors, it is ideal. There are, though, occasions and severe weather when wise Talitha appears keen to rally the nervous sisters, and once persuaded, with a resolute air, she shepherds her uncertain daughters inside the hotel to safety. In Talitha's protective presence, a warm piebald family can huddle happily together because they know: there's power in numbers – and mother's formidable right hook!

Occasionally Maria is brought indoors by the woman for an enforced retreat which she usually spends safely, resting quietly underneath a chair, when a knee is temporarily unavailable. Although she is very tough

and feisty, her bad habit of lying under hedges and in damp, unobtrusive places during autumn and winter, invariably results in her becoming run down and wheezy.

Even in falling snow she can be obstinate and intransigent: unwilling to abandon her love of the wild, open spaces: and as the flakes swirl thickly and change her coat from black and white to all white, still her edgy reluctance prevails, often for long, frustrating hours. Tucked out of reach but never out of sight, Maria's stubbornness will reach new heights. It is a test of patience and a long endurance battle, of slow (and wet!) persuasion on the woman's part, which is never easily won.

And as if able to read her mind and suspiciously aware of her intentions, Maria plays a game of hide and seek with the woman, darting here and there, into neighbour's gardens and inaccessible hidey holes until (sometimes after many hours), she finally surrenders. "Oh, maybe just for a quick warm then: it is feeling frosty now. Are there any prawns in the hotel I might have, do you think?"

Then, despite her initial, extreme reluctance, she will swiftly change and behave like a totally different cat. Once her resistance is thawed, she is a drooling, purring lap cat wanting undivided attention, constant stroking to her head, neck, stomach: in fact, nothing less than complete top to toe devotion is demanded! The constraint of worryingly closed doors is temporarily forgotten in her rapture as this fickle little friend retires briefly, but eventually willingly, from her cold outside world. All she asks is for a private litter tray, plenty of delicious food and an extra-large helping of love.

Having a very hearty appetite, Maria will happily relish any food little Lucy or her mother cannot manage. During winter, her demand for warmed drinks finds her rooted to the spot, tirelessly licking her mouth, waiting expectantly for that magic moment, communicating and anticipating her desire. On warm days Maria lazes for long, secretive hours, sharing an out-of-the-way, sun-warmed spot in a contented family threesome relaxing with Talitha and Lucy. At night, Maria's preference is usually to snuggle up and sleep inside the converted cupboard in the garden in her chosen bed on the top story. With its carpet, soft pillow and woollens, she happily tucks herself into the farthest, safest recess.

On her regular night-time hunts at the greenhouses in the Nursery, Maria is highly successful in stalking the mouse population: well-trained by her mother. Then she will proudly and carefully bring her small rodent trophies home as gifts, especially for the woman, left kindly for her at the door. Chester might be able to magically 'own' any of the other resident's mouse trophies, but he is never successful at pinching Maria's catch! Whatever her mood, whether she's ratty and reticent, or delightful and adorably affectionate, courageous Maria's got enough personality and love for two wonderful cats!

Winsome Lucy
The pretty cat with a problem

Click! Another photo snapped of the dreamy, dainty cat dozing among the flowering shrubs in the Garden Nursery: "Oooo! That's fabulous! I don't know when I saw a prettier little cat!" Or, at Christmas time, sitting casually surrounded by holly, mistletoe and a forest of spruce trees, again, another glowing exclamation: "That cat sitting there is just perfect! I think I've got my Christmas cards sorted!" And another splendid photo of Lucy was taken! Then later, as she was ambling along the path of the Cats' Hotel: "Mummy! Stop! Look! That cat over there is the loveliest I have ever seen anywhere!"

Another day passed, and if one cat in the Cats' Hotel caused more people to repeatedly stop and stare and say "Aaah!", "Sweeeet!", "Just SO cute!", or "Beautiful!", it was Lucy, always little Lucy. And gently going about things, it was generally believed, that with her gorgeous fur coat, petite frame and enchanting, pretty face, she deserved the recognition of strangers who can't help but admire – "She's just like a picture on an old-fashioned chocolate box!", as they view her from a little distance away!

A closer inspection is likely, however, to produce distinctly different remarks, because there is a terrible truth none of them know! Beneath the wonderful, pleasing first impression, lies a well-disguised defect: clouds of fluffy fur conceal terrible knots and tangles which present a constant problem for this diminutive outdoor cat. Inheriting a thick and beautiful coat from her mother, Lucy's fur is actually longer, and whereas Talitha, so grand, is always gloriously groomed, her daughter is invariably dishevelled.

Underneath that huge, furry overcoat is a miniature moggy with a massive problem. However hard she tries, there's no way Lucy can manage herself: with her little neck and tongue at full stretch, no amount of grooming can ever reach the end of her over-long coat. Luckily (and very unlike her sister Maria), Lucy can be relied upon to submit regularly when she needs a human's helping hand! Usually, she's quite relaxed and cooperative, and in spring and summer the woman has a well-versed routine. Sitting on a certain garden seat in the grounds, with scissors and comb in hand, of her own volition, lovely little Lucy comes too! Happily presenting herself for her beauty treatment, she obligingly says: "Time for my grooming appointment is it?" Compliant, and apparently very appreciative, she willingly yields to this assistance. Several times a week nasty knots will form in her fine hair and regular maintenance is inevitably required.

Though Lucy Darling (as the woman calls her small, unkempt friend), does have rather bad habits which are not exactly conducive in maintaining a perfect coat! Whereas her mother is controlled and serious, Lucy is naturally carefree, slightly frivolous and always happy. Completely in her element, she will delightedly roll about with abandoned joy in dusty soil and dead leaves!

A beauty session may have been just completed, the clumps of her discarded black and white fur cast to the wind for the birds to warmly line their nests, and as soon as she is transformed to tidiness, she's off! As if expressing relief and reckless merriment at her newly ordered, untangled loveliness, she will promptly frolic and wallow in flower borders or piles of twigs and garden debris. "I know you said I looked really stunning, but I'm just making myself feel right again!"

There are always those awkward, sensitive places, too: her armpits, between her legs and on her chest, where matted tufts quickly cultivate into small, hard furry lumps and ropy, knotted wodges. These inconvenient constrictions do present much more of a challenge. Of course, in winter she must have her grooming sessions inside, and despite this, Lucy is usually extremely patient. "I expect I do need it, but please, you won't be too long will you?" Staying still and uncomplaining, the snip, snip of the blunt-ended scissors will, she's aware, eventually release her from her tiresome restrictions.

For the woman it's never the same twice! Who knows what may be found lurking in those entangled places?! Seeds, twigs and bits of leaves are often embedded in Lucy's secret, taggy depths – but – there is a special reward! "Really", the woman says proudly, in satisfaction, "there is nothing more attractive and magical than a brooch made from a lock of Lucy's long fur, a stylish two-tone tuft!" Intriguing and original, many times they have provoked interest and comment, and each one is so wonderfully unique!

Little Lucy Darling is also very generous: often she will return with (slightly bedraggled) furry gifts she's found, her 'thank you', especially for the woman, laid neatly at the door! Well-trained by Taltha, Lucy is a highly dextrous mouser, and (so long as Chester doesn't spot her catch and claim it first as his due), it will be proudly presented as planned. Praising Lucy's proficiency, congratulations are always offered as well as profuse thanks, and then surreptitiously, the woman takes her gardening trowel, and digging a deep hole in the shade of the shrubbery, returns the poor mouse to nature.

Not nearly as nervous as Maria, Lucy's occasional slightly skittish insecurity indoors can be tempered by her delight in finding and frolicking with catnip mice, and although the sisters do have their own to play with outside, if the need arises, uncertainties can usually be successfully alleviated in this way.

During summer when the catnip grown in the garden, is flourishing, most of the cats are thrilled, but none more obviously so than little Lucy. Rolling about and cavorting in the border, chewing, drooling and rubbing in her delight, Lucy is capriciously enraptured. Relaxed and dreamily contented, a drowsy sleep then beckons: minor things like grooming debris from fur can always wait until later for Lucy!

With rather short legs, the length of Lucy's coat, combined with her predilection for the over-grown, wildest places, results in a grubby and sometimes damp, but happy cat. Apart from the issues with her coat, Lucy is always in good health, brightly alert, but never as clean as any of the other cats!

Never greedy, and slowly enjoying all her meals outdoors (except in very heavy rain or snow), Lucy will then either eat in her favoured alternative quarters, the outbuilding, or underneath a large pink, summer parasol erected especially to keep her dry. With her dainty, furry feet and toes and fantastically dense coat, fortunately, Lucy doesn't appear to ever feel the cold. Despite this she does favour a big basket for her bed, well-lined with a sheepskin blanket and woollens. Little Lucy likes a long lie-in which is never disturbed. Knowing her night times are industriously spent mousing by moonlight, which might have kept her busy till late, the humans completely understand.

When the special, occasional treat of a pan of fish for all the cats is cooking, Lucy sits at the back door and enthusiastically sings – along with the other fish fans in the kitchen – in mutual, eager anticipation. With a very marked difference to her mother's taste, Lucy's habitual preference is to relish a little fresh titbit of grilled kipper at the weekend. Also, her sociable, easy going nature is quite the opposite of her unpredictable (sometimes surly) sister Maria, or the rather reserved and reticent Talitha.

Sounding at times more like a baby lamb bleating, blithe Lucy's high, loud mew makes sure her appealing voice is always heard. And never displaying any sort of aggression, her loving, playful, companionable disposition, ensures delightful Lucy Darling is much-loved and admired in return, by all cats and people alike.

The Cats' Hotel Series

If you enjoyed your visit to **The Cats' Hotel**,
the fifteen books are all available as separate ebooks:

Lively Leonora, Our fickle, friendly extrovert
Gentle Jasper, Our precious, brave guardian
Reserved Roland, The dreamer with hidden depths
Melancholy Marley, The most marvellous mother
Nifty Tufty, Mistress of subtle surprise
Tenacious Tuppence, The cat who was left behind
Badger Brock, The magical cat with a secret life
Wonderful Woody, The tiny kitten who grew and grew
Intrepid Elfie, The fearless explorer
Clever Chester, The cat who can tell the time
Filthy Wilfy, The cat who can't keep clean
Squeaky Chiki, The solitary singer
Queen Talitha, The regal cat of humble birth
Moody Maria, The quirky cat with two personalities
Winsome Lucy, The pretty cat with a problem

About the author and illustrator
Pamela Blanchfield

My earliest memories involve drawing, being outside and cats, and I was lucky to grow up in a Victorian house with a large garden and my own wood.

I was friendly with the fourteen cats who also lived there, but none of them were 'mine'.

I knew when I grew up this would change, and I was right! I still love art and gardening and especially all of the cats who have made their way to The Cats' Hotel.

Printed in Great Britain
by Amazon